ALSO BY BEN K. GREEN

HORSE TRADIN' (1967)

*THIS IS A BORZOI BOOK,
PUBLISHED IN NEW YORK BY ALFRED A. KNOPF*

WILD COW TALES

WILD

ALFRED·A·KNOPF·New York·1969

COW TALES

by BEN K. GREEN

illustrated by LORENCE BJORKLUND

THIS IS A BORZOI BOOK
PUBLISHED BY ALFRED A. KNOPF, INC.

First Edition
Copyright © 1969 by Ben K. Green
All rights reserved under International and
Pan-American Copyright Conventions. Published
in the United States by Alfred A. Knopf, Inc.,
New York, and simultaneously in Canada by
Random House of Canada Limited, Toronto.
Distributed by Random House, Inc., New York.
Library of Congress Catalog Card Number: 68–23940
Manufactured in the United States of America

CONTENTS

WILD COW TALES

INTRODUCTION

THERE WAS A TIME IN THE LATE 1920's and early 1930's when very few teen-age boys or young men had any aspirations to be cowboys. The Machine Age was fast taking the day and young men were learning trades in keeping with progress and changing times. There was little or no glamour attached to the cattle business during this period and cowboys were looked upon either as ruffians or individuals with less mentality than it took to adjust to the Machine Age.

After the crash in 1929 cattle were of very little value and many ranchers, both large and small, went out of business and there was no way for a day-labor cowboy to make a living. Men with families and responsibilities had to learn some other trade, and the only young men that would still ride for a living, handle cattle, and break horses were those that had no desire to do anything else regardless of what they might be paid because of their love of cowboyin'.

Bankers hated to see a cowboy come in the bank for a loan, and if you were a cowboy, your best friends would have rather waved at you than to have been caught talking to you. As far as I was personally concerned, being a horseman and a cowboy was a disease and no treatment would have done any good. If they had a vaccine for it, it wouldn't have taken on me. My high-school classmates referred to me as being backward and nonprogressive, and for the most part may have felt a little sorry for me. In spite of all this, I preferred to stay in the cow business, live horseback, and be independent of any source of income that would deprive me of my time and personal liberties.

I started out being a cowboy when I crawled out of the cradle, and I had never gotten used to very many of the luxuries that most people considered necessities. Camping out in rough country under a bluff or close to a windmill had never occurred to me as being anything but normal living, and I didn't understand what most people referred to as hardships in camp living.

Cattle were cheap and wild cattle were worth about half as much as cattle that could be handled horseback. This being true, one of the ways that I had of surviving the financial strains of the times and staying in the cattle business was to buy or handle for other people outlaw cattle that, if and when I could catch them, would make me more money than the meager amount that could be made in the handling of ordinary cattle at the prices they were bringing.

All Western cattle might have been referred to by farmers or Midwestern cattle feeders as being wild, and it's true that cattle were far from being gentle from the standpoint of allowing a man to work among them horseback or on foot. Cattle that would booger at the sight of a man or any of the common mechanical sounds of modern civilization and break to run for cover would be the kind of cattle that cowboys referred to as being wild.

Outlaw cattle are those that have gotten away from main herds on roundups, one or several times, and have learned to hide in dense brush, river bottoms or mountainous country. Such cattle learn how to get away from a rider and if they are cornered will try to fight their way out and it seems that it becomes their purpose to stay in whatever particular part of a range where they have the most protection and are least likely to be roped or driven.

The reader will understand that all of the accounts in *Wild Cow Tales* will have some similarities since each account of trapping wild cattle has its setting in some type of rough country where cattle can hide or can get away because a rider cannot follow or head them at top speed over rough terrain, brush, logs, or some other obstacles.

I have gathered thousands of cattle that represented no more than tired horses and torn clothes. The accounts in this book are the unusual circumstances and the original tricks that I had to use to outsmart outlaw cattle and keep my reputation as a top cowhand.

COUNTRY
COW
BUYER

COUNTRY COW BUYERS, IT COULD BE said, were a product of the times in which they flourished. In the late 1920's and early 1930's, trucks and trailers were not in common use by farmers and small ranchers. In the livestock-farming regions of Texas (es-

pecially along the rivers where the farms had been put in valleys and the ridges and hills were still left in grasslands), the livestock farmer would be running a few head of cattle and raising some calves to sell. He'd also have some cull cows to get rid of occasionally, and now and then a mean fightin' bull that wouldn't stay at home, or other breechy cattle ("breechy" meaning cattle that wouldn't stay inside of a fence) that he'd need to sell. It took about forty head of mixed cattle to make a carload, which would necessitate a number of small stockmen puttin' their cattle together for a shipment, which never was a very satisfactory arrangement. This situation developed country cow buyers.

I started by hirin' out horseback, helpin' country cow buyers when they'd go out and throw cattle together from several different owners until they had enough for a carload. Then we'd drive 'em into town and ship 'em by rail to Fort Worth, Texas. I was a young cowboy, high-school age, when I started buyin' cattle for myself, especially durin' the summer months. It was mid-July and all the country cattle had gotten fat on summer grass; and now was the time to start ridin' the rivers and the ridges to buy what was commonly referred to as "jackpot" cattle. I saddled my horse late that Sunday afternoon, tied a small bedroll and a little grub on the back of my saddle, and headed south to the Brazos River to see if I could put together a load of cattle.

On trips a country cow buyer never planned on campin' out much. I usually spent the night with people that I was doin' business with or old friends, and many of the families would have boys and girls about my age.

Country cow buyers were always welcome to spend the night, stop by to eat, and were generally well respected because they were the means of the small stock farmer sellin' his odd lots of cattle—and, then too, we carried the news. Radios were scarce, telephones were not too common, and about the only newspapers were brought by the mail carrier once a week. This made ever'body glad to see you and want to find out what was goin' on in town and from communities you had last ridden through.

The first night out I spent with the Weaver family. They had a boy, Mike, who was a little bit younger than I, and his sister, Pam, was about my age. We all knew each other, but Mike and Pam went to school in the country and I went to school in town. They were just sort of passing acquaintances of mine.

When I rode up just before dark, Mike and ever'body hollered get down and come in and that kind of welcome stuff. But Mr. Weaver, lookin' to the practical side of things, said, "Ben, unsaddle your horse and put him in the barn and feed him. You know we are not goin' to let you ride on any further—you've got to spend the night with us."

Mr. Weaver and I got my horse put away and went back to the house. Mrs. Weaver and Pam were puttin' supper on the table. Country gardens were in their flush of production and spring chickens had had time to get fryin'-size; and this bein' Sunday night, we had a big supper—it looked like without anybody half tryin' to fix it so. We set out on the porch awhile after dark and visited, talked about ever'thing in general, and, of course, our own business in particular. Mr. Weaver told me that he had five yearlings and a fat, dry cow that he wanted to sell me the next mornin'. However, it was the custom of good country people not to discuss business much on Sunday, even if it was after dark. Mike had chimed in and said if I was goin' to be gone down the road a few days that he might have a steer or two caught for me when I got back. This all made interestin' conversation and pretty soon we went to bed.

It was hot summertime and I slept out in the yard on a pallet with Mike. We got up about daylight; ever'body was gonna have lots to do durin' the day. Mike and his daddy wanted to get to the field, and Pam and her mother were gonna start cannin', and I needed to get on down the road and hunt cattle to buy. We looked at the yearlings and the fat cow when I went to the barn with 'em to do the morning feedin'; and, of course, I didn't have much trouble buyin' these cattle. It was the custom of the country to ride by and buy cattle and leave them until you had bought enough for a carload and then you turned back and threw 'em together and started drivin' 'em towards town.

Cattle were plentiful, but they were all doin' real good and nearly ever'body wanted to keep their calves until they were bigger and sell 'em to me that fall. So it took me all week to buy a load of the odd head here and yonder that were ready to be sold. It was late Saturday afternoon before I got back across the Brazos River and up to the Weavers.

Other members of the family were still out in the field, but Mike was in the shade of the trees in the front yard settin' in the swing with his right leg in a cast. I pushed my cattle on up the road past the house where they could graze. It was late in the afternoon and it wasn't any trouble to get 'em to stop and graze.

I rode up in the yard and stepped off my horse and said, "Mike, what happened to you?"

He said, "Well, I don't guess I'll have you any extra steers because I roped one of 'em, he jerked my horse down on me and broke my leg, and the rope came off the saddle horn after my horse fell and the steer got away."

I said, "Mike, you're graduatin' from a farm boy to a cowboy 'cause you don't make a cowboy until you get a leg or two or sumpin' broke, either by wild cattle or bad horses."

This didn't seem to console him much, and he just put on a weak grin and said, "Maybe so."

While he was explainin' to me how it all happened, the rest of the family came in from the field, and after we all had our howdies, Pam spoke up and said, "Mike, have you remembered your manners enough to tell Ben that we want him to spend the night with us?"

And, of course, he hadn't, so his remark was, "Ben don't have to be told. He knows he can spend the night here."

I said, "Well, I don't know what I'm gonna do with my cattle unless I just let 'em bed down in the grass along the side of the road." This wasn't too uncommon a practice to let cattle bed along the road; and if you'd driven 'em pretty hard all day, they wouldn't drift too far before mornin'.

Mr. Weaver again spoke up and told me that I could drive 'em up the road to the first field and turn 'em in the gate where he had already finished threshing his oats and that there'd be enough pickin's around the edges of the oat stubble for the cattle to fill up durin' the night. And the next mornin' we could put the cattle that I bought from him with them.

This all sounded good and didn't take but a little while to tend to. We had a nice supper and a good visit and I gave 'em the news of several families on down below the river that they knew. One girl had sent a new pattern book by me to Pam. And another item of news was that there was gonna be an all-day singin' at their church next Sunday, and ever'body I saw had told me to be sure and tell the Weavers to come. This was the sort of thing that made country cow buyers worth their keep to country people.

While we were settin' on the porch that night, Mike's daddy explained how come Mike to rope the big steer and break his own leg. There had been some Fort Worth cowmen that were in the livestock commission business on the Fort Worth stockyards, and one of 'em was a cattle buyer for a packin' company on the Fort Worth stockyards that had leased some pasture land on the old Kuteman Ranch. When they moved their cattle out they lost five big steers that had gotten out into the Brazos River bottom; several cowboys had tried to catch 'em. Mike wanted to make some extra money and had gone over into the river bottom and jumped one of these big steers, and got into the storm, and after dark Mr. Weaver and a neighbor had gotten uneasy when Mike didn't return and had gone over there and found him layin' under

a tree on the riverbank with a leg broke, waitin' for somebody to come hunt him.

The story was that the Fort Worth cowmen were
offerin' $10 a head for anybody that'ould catch these
steers and had offered to sell 'em, range delivery, but
hadn't any takers on their range-delivery proposition.
Mike didn't have much idea about what these cattle
would weigh, but Mr. Weaver had seen one or two of 'em
at a distance and said they were about three- to four-year-
old steers and might weigh as much as 900 to 1,000
pounds per head.

Pam and her mother gave me some messages for people farther up the road and also a small list of thread and
stuff for me to take to a store in town and they'd send it
out on the mail hack. I got my cattle throwed together
and started up the road with 'em the next mornin' a little
after sunup.

When a man's buyin' cattle and puttin' 'em in a herd
and they're all strange to each other, ever'time he puts in
a fresh one there's a few fights. They don't drive good
together, they don't follow a leader, and they're always
lookin' for a break in the fences along the road or a
chance to turn down a blind lane. When you come to a
country plank bridge with a few holes in it or maybe a
whole plank out, you've got a real batch of cow work to
do. There's never been any ranch work or rodeo perform-
ances that would ever teach a horse what he will have to
know if you're gonna use him for a jackpot cow horse.

A country cow buyer's horse has to be good. First, he
must have a nice way of travelin' to get you down the

road and over the country, then he needs to have a good rein, lots of cow sense, and endowed with more than a common amount of patience, together with an unbelievable amount of real stamina, for a cow buyer to ever get back to town on him with a roadful of mixed cattle.

As I drove my cattle up the road, I kept thinkin' about those five big steers. The Kuteman Ranch was not leased to anybody and the five wild steers were in there away from any other cattle. As I drove along I decided that I would turn into the first gate on the Kuteman Ranch and drift my cattle down through the river-bottom pasture and came out on the Balch Road, which ran north and south on the east side of the Kuteman pasture. I could still turn north and go into town, and it wouldn't be much more than another half-day drive. Wild steers just might come bawlin' and pawin' dirt over their back and fight with these strange cattle of mine while I just drove 'em on out into the road.

I knew I'd be takin' a pretty big chance of gettin' out on the other side of the ranch with all my cattle because they weren't stayin' together too good anyway. This didn't bother me too much; I was ridin' the best horse I ever owned—mare named Beauty—and she could tell what a cow was thinkin' about, with the cow on the other side of the pasture. I turned the cattle into the Kuteman pasture and drove about halfway across the ranch without seein' or hearin' any kind of cattle. There was a creek ran out of the pasture and down into the Brazos River at the east side of the ranch that was covered with plenty of good grass and shade. I was lettin' these cattle graze and driftin' 'em about as slow as I could for two reasons:

lettin' them fill up would keep them quiet and easier to drive, and it'd give these wild steers more time to locate them.

As the cattle grazed into the glad on the creek bank, two big red steers bounced out of the bush, threw their heads up, and wrung their tails and bawled real loud like wild, bad cattle will do when they're surprised but not scared. I stopped and let 'em mill into my cattle, and sure 'nuff they started a bawlin', dirt-throwin' cow fight! It was just a matter of seconds until the other three steers came out of the brush and joined 'em. I didn't holler or whistle or make any smart cowboy noises. I rode up slow enough to keep the cow fight and the cow grazin' movin' towards the other side of the pasture without makin' any show that I was interested in breakin' up the fight or hurryin' up the drive.

In about a half an hour these cattle were all grazin' along slow together and just occasionally one of 'em would make a run at the other one. I took a long way around and stayed in the brush, got out in front of 'em, and opened the gate into the road. Then I dropped back in the thicket and waited for the cattle to work themselves out into the open, which must have been about another hour or so. As they got up close to the gate, some old, fat, dry milk cows (that I had bought from farmers) that are always inquisitive about an open gate started out into the road. They turned the wrong direction down the road back towards the river, but I wasn't gonna let that unnerve me until they all went through that gate; then I could shut the gate and have a little race with 'em down that road a mile or two if I had to go that far to turn 'em back. A lone cowboy with a bunch of cattle always welcomes the possibility of gettin' his herd between two fences down a lane. But I did better'n this. I shut the gate and ran down the inside of the fence horseback until I got past the herd, then I got down afoot, crawled through fence, and drove the cattle back up the road afoot. Ole Beauty followed the fence line and me and the cattle back up to the gate where I let her out and got back on her and started to drive to town with five more big steers that I hadn't paid for yet. I didn't even know whether I could buy 'em or not, and if I didn't get to the Fort Worth owners before someone else did I might be accused of stealing them.

It was a little after high noon Sunday, and I was about ten miles from town. With good luck I figured I might make it to the railroad stock pens a little before dark, and if there was a car available (sometimes you had to order stockcars several days in advance) I could load these cattle out that night and they'd be on the Fort Worth market Monday morning.

The day wasn't much too hot and these cattle traveled pretty good. I sent word to town by a fellow that passed in a car to a coupla cowboys to meet me in the edge of town and help me through town to the stock pens. And sure 'nuff about five o'clock they rode into sight, and we had just begun to go up South Main, where there were people and yards and flowerbeds and clotheslines and sidewalks and kids playin', and lots of other stuff that didn't help cow drivin' none. But with a minor amount of chousing the cattle and it bein' Sunday we didn't get too much cussin' for crossin' people's yards, and we made it to the stock pens about an hour before dark.

Railroad agents in those days, so far

as cowboys were concerned, weren't exactly God's most noble chillun. They were independent and hateful and wore long black sleeves to keep their shirts clean and green-billed eye shades that made 'em look more yellow than they already were. They carried big watches on long chains to look at often instead of answering you when you asked 'em what time the next cow train would be in. Along the Texas-Pacific Railroad, they kept the stock pens locked until you rode up to the depot and took your hat off and begged 'em for a key.

Well, I'd gone through all this lotsa times. So I went up to argue with whoever and ever'body that was there about gettin' a car to load that night. And I heard all kinds of reasons and excuses why they couldn't spot a car on such short notice. So me and my cowboy friends tied our saddle horses onto an empty stockcar and took pinch bars and pulled and worked it down the railroad track even with the loadin' chute. It's little stunts like this that could be cited to railroad stockholders to explain to them what happened to a lot of their cow business.

I caught a passenger train to Fort Worth about midnight, and my cowboy friends loaded my cattle about three o'clock in the morning on a train that would get the cattle to Fort Worth in time for the Monday-morning market. When I got off the train in Fort Worth I took a streetcar out North Main to Exchange Avenue where I sat around the old Stockyards Hotel dining room and ate and drank and visited with the boys that drifted in and out until about daylight. I went up to the Livestock Exchange Building, and there were a few people showin' up for the day's business and the stockyards had about filled up with cattle. In a little while comes the commission man that owned the five steers, and I saw him go upstairs to open his office. I had always shipped my cattle to Daggett and Keene Commission Company, but I had billed out the car to this man's commission company before I got on the train. I followed him into his office and there were a few other people that came in at the same time, and the day's work was about to start.

Then he turned and looked at me and said, "Do you want to see me?"

I said, "Yes, sir. I wondered if you wanted to sell me the five steers, range delivery, in the Kuteman pasture."

Well this sure broke the ice on that ole boy. He reached up and opened the swingin' door that separated the loafin' part of the office from the business part of the office and shook hands with me and went to playin' like he thought he knew me. While we were talkin' about the big steers, a man walked down the hall that he hollered at to come in; he was the packer buyer that was his partner on the cattle. He told him what my mission was, and they'as in a hurry to explain to me that they could catch the cattle. That it wouldn't be any trouble, but that they just hadn't had time. And that they was awful busy so they guessed they'd sell 'em to me. They wanted to lead me to believe that it wasn't because the cattle was wild, it was just because they was such big operators that they didn't have time to go catch 'em.

I listened to all of this and waited for 'em to tell me how much they'd take for 'em. They said they hadn't seen 'em in a year, but that they thought they ought to be worth $40 a head.

This Mr. Packer Buyer spoke up and said, "Well, if my partner will take that for 'em, I will, but it sounds awful cheap to me." He went on to say that the demand for big steers was real good and if they were on the stock-yards that mornin' they'd be worth eight cents a pound!

'Course him and Mr. Commission Man knew there wasn't a chance for them wild steers to be on the stock-yard that morning and that speech was meant to make me buy 'em at $40 a head. Well, I knew that was $200 for five head, and I was writin' 'em out a check for the money and had told 'em that I was going to buy the cattle, range delivery. Mr. Packer Buyer was reassuring me that it was a smart buy, and that if they was on the stockyards that morning he would be glad to give eight cents a pound for 'em. I handed the commission man the $200 check and I asked him did he want to call the bank on my check. He said, No, sir. My check was good with him and that I had just bought and paid for five steers.

About that time the train whistle blew and there was a cattle train bein' spotted, and the crew was about to start unloadin' 'em into the stock pens.

I turned to Mr. Commission Man and said, "I con-signed you a load of cattle that were shipped out of Weatherford last night, and they're unloadin' 'em now out there in the stock pens." As I looked out the winder I said, "If you'll look right quick you can see those five steers comin' down the chute, and I'm instructing you to weigh 'em to Mr. Packer Buyer for eight cents a pound."

BEEF

CATTLE, PEOPLE, AND THE DIETS
of both have undergone revolutionary changes since the
turn of the century. In the early days of the cattle industry
the production of beef in the Western and Southwestern
regions of the United States was carried on by cattlemen
in such a way that big beef steers could be produced on
open range and fattened on the nutritious virgin grasses
with the least possible expense without the use of any
domestic feed grains. Another source of beef came from
big aged cows that had failed to produce a calf and
thereby had gotten fat and were considered to be excellent
beef. Fat cows were generally butchered by local meat
markets whereas big steers were usually driven and
shipped to local and Northern central markets.

Aged beef can mean two different things. When a

cowman refers to aged beef he means cattle that have
reached maturity and are no longer growing additional
carcass and are fattened on the grass. To a packer, pro-
cessor, or today's housewife aged beef can mean beef that
has been made from cattle slaughtered at any age,
weight, or size, and the aging process referred to here is
the length of time and the temperature that the beef has
been aged in storage—but this is not the original meaning
of the term "aged beef." By the different use of the same
wording much confusion can be caused among today's
modern amateurs in the discussion of beef.

In my days of growing up we worked outdoors in the
wintertime and ate much more beef and pork than we did
in the summertime. Pork was not considered good summer diet and in those days we never learned to use or
knew what the word "diet" meant. People living in hot climates and working in the summer sun are more comfortable and withstand the heat better when they eat beef.

Refrigeration has been a contributing factor in changing the meat supply to the human race. It was a common
practice on ranches, cow camps, and even in large families to hang a big aged beef, dressed, up in the top of the
windmill tower, especially in the wintertime. By the use
of pulleys and ropes the side of beef would be let down to
arm's level and the day's supply would be sliced off whatever part of the carcass that was being eaten at the time.
The remaining part would be hoisted back into the top of
the windmill tower above the level of the ground insects,
such as flies and so forth, where the air would cause a
crust to form around the meat and keep it for several
weeks in perfect condition. A more humid climate might

cause several ranches or several families to adopt the practice of taking time about butchering a beef and distributing it among several families in order that it be eaten up before it spoiled in the absence of refrigeration.

Another means of protecting meat was by constructing what was referred to as a screen house. Such a building would be located where there was usually a breeze and would have a roof and be closed in all the way around with screen wire to let the air blow freely, and with the exception of the very hottest of weather, this was a satisfactory way in dry climates to protect fresh meat for several days until it could be used.

I remember, as a boy, when the only known refrigeration in the Southwest was manufactured ice. (In the North people cut ice and put it in their own ice houses to be used in the summer.) Ice was not made in every community; only large towns and cities had ice factories, and the ice was shipped in freight carloads to smaller communities. Most iceboxes in the home were homemade and had doubled walls. The best ones were lined on the inside with flat galvanized sheet iron and the two or three inches spaced between the walls were packed with cottonseed hulls or sawdust and had heavy lids made of the same construction to fit these iceboxes. Manufactured refrigerators that stood upright and had doors that opened from the side with a separate compartment for ice were owned by people that were thought of as being well-to-do, and these iceboxes were almost prestige symbols. Of course with either kind the ice melted faster when we kids opened and slammed the doors.

We lived at the edge of the small town of Cumby,

which boasted two meat markets. These meat markets had what were called walk-in iceboxes, and the ice was hoisted overhead with a block and tackle and put in the top compartment; these refrigerators were no more nor no less effective for the purpose used than the home ice-boxes, which meant that the local meat market operator butchered beef several times a week in order not to take any chances on it spoiling from this damp, imperfect sort of refrigeration.

Steak was the common diet for breakfast in the sum-mertime. I slept on the porch all summer as a kid and kept my pony in a grass patch next to the yard. I would have preferred to have kept my pony in the yard where she could nuzzle her soft nose around on me in my sleep but my family had some kind of peculiar ideas about sanitation and keeping horses in the yard. However, I overcame this handicap when I went to cowboy'n' and batch'n'. My first chore in the morning was to get up before the rest of the family and hop on my pony bare-back and lope to town and get the steak for breakfast. Some people of course walked to the meat market, but there would be half a dozen other kids horseback that had loped to town to get steak for breakfast and the old meat market man would look out the door and see us waiting on our ponies and knew who we were, how many were in our families, how thick or thin our mothers wanted the meat cut, and pretty soon he would come out the screen door with his apron rolled up and hand us our separate packages of meat, and we would lope off home for breakfast. Needless to say, a kid sleeping on the porch in the open air, riding a pony a mile before breakfast thought steak for breakfast was just the thing.

The meat in local markets would be from the carcass of barren cows or steers that weighed around 1,000 pounds and were thought of as lightweight, local-butchering-type cattle. Big steers that were shipped fat off the grass to supply the cities trade and especially Eastern markets were seldom ever weighed in at the packers under 1,400 pounds and 1,600-pound steers were ideal and thought to be more or less common to the finer trade. When T-bone, sirloin, or any of the better cuts were served in hotels or restaurants, all the tallow was cooked with the red meat and served on the platter. There was no air conditioning, very little if any so-called central heat, and closed automobiles referred to as sedans were barely making their appearance and we ate big heavy fat beef to supply energy to walk where we were going and the heat to maintain our bodies in bad weather. In all our ignorance the human race had not discovered vitamins and knew very little about minerals, food supplements, and so forth, and had we all stayed on a solid diet of aged beef, fresh vegetables and tree-ripened fruits, natural sun-ripened and carefully harvested cereal grains, it is just possible we might have never discovered the blessing of vitamins and other food supplements.

During this period of the development of the cattle industry, it is true that some aged steers were fattened in the Corn Belt states and corn-fed cattle were considered by some people to be superior beef to grass-finished cattle of the same age.

So-called milk-fed calf, baby beef and veal, was scorned as being a poor substitute for meat. Baby beef might be served at a ladies' luncheon but men scorned the stuff as a poor substitute for something to eat.

The transportation and living conditions of Americans began to change right after World War I to the extent that there developed a small demand for what was considered to be lightweight beef, meaning under one thousand pounds live weight. This trend was very gradual because people's living habits still required a great deal of physical effort and hard food was still cherished and soft diets had not become the order of the day. Big steers and big-steer operators still enjoyed the major portion of the demand for beef. With much promotion on the part of cattle feeders and cattle breeders, baby beef began to make some inroads on the big-beef market. Land was continually increasing in value and the breaking up of large ranches had begun in an almost unnoticed way.

By the late 1920's production costs had begun to make it less profitable to keep steers and other beef animals until they were several years old. Most of the people in America had begun to ride in automobiles and were burning less protein foods, and lightweight cattle had gotten into major demand. The crash of 1929 broke the buying power of the purchasing public and a cutoff of a small beef was far more in reach of the average consumer and the luxury living class of Americans that had insisted on and demanded big finished beef was dwindling to a very small number. Big steers broke just about all the cattlemen that were specializing in them alone, and the cattle producers that survived had to change their operations to lightweight beef; the demand for baby beef and veal, which is a sucking calf that weighs less than 300 pounds, comprised most of the beef-tonnage turnover.

Young cattle in their growing years do not put on enough tallow under most grazing operations to produce a good quality of meat when slaughtered. The cry for quality at light weight stimulated the cattle-feeding business because young cattle had to be confined in feed lots on concentrated feed grains and protein such as cottonseed meal, soybean meal, etc., in order to fatten in spite of their growing age.

Cattlemen had been improving the fleshing qualities of their breeding stock for several generations and the so-called beef specialists from our various agricultural universities sponsored and demanded in the show ring a lightweight, heavy-fleshed, highly finished young animal and brought on the feeding and exhibiting of baby beef animals by our boys and girls that were studying animal husbandry and agriculture at all levels of education. Breeders, in order to satisfy the modern demand, were forced to breed square, blocky, short-legged, heavy-fleshed cattle that in reality and fact were less adaptive to the cattle grass ranches of the range country, and cattle of such conformation would naturally produce less milk for their offspring.

This trend for compact, smooth, showy feeder cattle in the course of twenty-five years has almost destroyed the practical purposes of large livestock in that, with their lack of milk and their burdensome conformation, such cattle are not capable of foraging over a wide range making a living as well as producing a big calf. I well remember when the first beef specialists were sent out to advise cattlemen as to how to improve and breed smooth,

typy, modern beef cattle. Before this time when we rode
on a roundup it was necessary to ride to the top of the
mountains, the bottom of the canyons, and the further-
most corners of a big pasture because range cattle then
would be scattered and taking the best advantage of the
most country within a fenced pasture, regardless of how
large the pasture might be. Within three or four generations of crossing our good native range cattle with
European breeds of bulls, I began to notice, as a cowboy
and by then a rancher, that cattle didn't graze as far up
the mountain or as far from water and that range cows
seldom ever had enough milk, that one had to be roped
and milked when the calf was small to keep her bag from
spoiling.

By the early 1950's this clamor for baby beef, short,
compact breeding stock, and from using the advice of
educated specialists, cattle were so greatly improved that
during winter feeding time or during drought they would
meet you in the flat part of the pasture between the
windmill and the feed trough and, needless to say, the
struggle to try to make money off of such unproductive
cattle with the constantly climbing overhead put the cattle industry as a whole in the category of a poor business
that for the most part had to be subsidized by oil wells or
some other source of income derived from outside the
livestock industry. Cattlemen that through their stubborn-
ness had stayed with crossbreed cattle still had cows that
produced milk and raised big calves. This sort of operator
was ofttimes condemned by the brilliant, educated specialists of the animal kingdom because of his cattle's lack
of uniformity in color or some other characteristic that

would not affect the weight of the cattle and would have no effect on the beef and, in fact, would be some criticism of no material consequence.

By the beginning of the 1940's the American way of life had been modified by modern conveniences, easy modes of travel and air conditioning, to where the human appetite rebelled at the taste of excessive tallow or other fats. The modern housewife began to demand lighter cuts of beef with enough finish to ensure flavor and easy preparation in cooking and at the same time that the meat be trimmed of all excessive tallow and other waste materials such as cartilage, excessive bone, and so forth.

Tallow that is being trimmed from beef that sells for as much as a dollar a pound or more must be sold as waste for as little as seven cents a pound. This situation has caused packers to heavily penalize overfinished, overfat cattle that carry too much tallow, and today's trend in breeding cattle is to try to select breeding stock that will have a good growth factor and produce cattle that will gain economically to a point of light finish and will dress out with a minimum amount of waste with the maximum amount of red meat.

Lightweight young beef will be softer, which in a sense may be considered more tender, and it is true that this kind of meat is juicier than some of the best beef from heavy cattle. This juice cooks out very fast and beef from young cattle shrinks extremely much in cooking as compared to beef from aged cattle. To those who know, the flavor and food value of meat from young lightweight cattle is far inferior to the high quality of beef from older cattle. However, it will be hard for people of this generation and generations to come to miss something they have never had.

The next twenty years will be marked by numerous mistakes and failures before the ideal beef-type animal that is acceptable to the breeder, feeder, packer, and the housewife will be produced.

THE ONE
THAT
GOT AWAY

I WAS LATE SUMMER AND I HAD BE-
gun to put some lightweight heifers in the feed lot to
feed during the fall and winter months before and after
school. This feed-lot deal of mine was not very big. I
would feed forty or fifty head and send them to Fort

Worth in small truckloads as these certain individuals got fat enough to send to market. (About five cattle would fill a truck.)

This was sort of a new trick in the cattle-feeding business. Anybody that had a feed lot close to the Fort Worth market could take advantage of using this trucking way of gettin' cattle to town. By being able to send just a few head at a time, it was not necessary to overfeed the fattest ones waiting for the others to get fat enough to make up a full carload, and too, the same trucks could haul a few back from Fort Worth to go into the feed lot. It made the feeder's operation a more continuous kind of turnover in the cattle-feeding business and gave a small feeder like me a chance to make a little more money.

I had the east half of the old Lovelady Wagonyard in Weatherford leased for a feed lot. There was a short-haired cherry-red heifer in the last truckload of cattle that I had brought from Fort Worth. This little heifer refused to get up to the feed trough and eat, and she walked the fence and bawled two straight days and nights. The third morning when I came down to feed, things were noticeably quiet, and when I glanced over the lot, I realized that the little dark-red heifer was gone. The gates were still fastened and there were no breaks in the plank fence and no sign of how she got out. I made a few inquiries around the Silas Kemp Wagonyard and over at Dorsey Grain Company behind the feed lot, but nobody had seen my heifer.

The way you hunt stray cattle or stray horses if you know the lay of the land is to go to the spot that you think you would go if you were a stray heifer.

When I finished feedin', I started ridin' out Town Creek up the railroad right of way that ran parallel to the creek and out through the west end of town. There was always plenty of fresh spring water in the creek and green grass up and down the banks and this by late summer would be an ideal place for a stray heifer. My hunch wasn't too bad wrong because I picked up her track where she had drank, but she wasn't stoppin' to graze— she was travelin' west, and when she hit the fence line in the west end of town where there wasn't any more open land, she had drifted along the fence south to a public road that went west to the town of Garner.

I met Henry Clark comin' to town in a wagon. We visited a few minutes, and he told me that the heifer passed his house about daylight, when he was out at the barn by the road tendin' to his stock. This was the first man that had seen my heifer and the distance he lived from town meant that she had gotten out about three or four o'clock in the morning.

I picked up her track along the side of the road and her tracks showed she was steppin' out pretty fast and still not stoppin' to graze. Public country roads many times followed fence lines with the curve of a pasture or a field, and this road made a big, wide curve about three quarters of a mile and then turned back to the same generally westerly direction. The red heifer was goin' west and had her mind made up about it. Her tracks showed very plainly where she had come to the curve in the road and jumped the fence.

I took the staples a-loose and pushed the wire down and stepped my horse over the wire. I let the wire back up and tied it to the post—no real damage done—and followed her tracks, thinkin' that she might be turnin' back towards a creek that ran back towards the north. As I followed her tracks up to the road on the other side of the wide curve she had jumped back over the fence where the road had turned due west, and I let the fence down in the same manner as the first one and picked up her tracks in the soft dirt of the gravel road.

A little before noon I rode in to Mr. Vance's store at Garner. I knew Mr. Vance well; he was a fine old country merchant and a gentleman of the old school who was interested in his community and the welfare of his neighbors.

I got a cold Coke out of the icebox, bought a box of cookies, and was talkin' to Mr. Vance and tellin' him about my heifer when a cute little cotton-headed girl maybe five years old came runnin' in at the back door of the store. She didn't talk plain enough to say "Mr. Vance" but she said something that sounded like it, and her face was all a-beam and her bright blue eyes were wide and joyful as she blared out, "Mr. Bance, Reddy Calf com'd home!"

Mr. Vance shot a quick glance at me and went to talking to the little girl and pattin' her on the head and tellin' her very gently that he was sure glad that her Reddy Calf had come home. With this she dashed out the back door and ran across the lot to a rather run-down little old house that the front porch was almost level with the ground.

Another cotton-headed girl maybe ten years old was feedin' Reddy Calf cornbread out of a pan and a baby girl maybe two years old was sittin' on top of Reddy Calf, and the one that had spread the news had run back and was combing the switch of Reddy Calf's tail. I watched a few minutes and my cookies tasted like sand and my Coke turned sour. I must have had a bewildered look on my face when Mr. Vance began to explain that these were motherless little girls that their father was trying to raise and make a living for; someone had given them Reddy Calf as a baby and they had raised it for a pet. Mr. Vance looked away from me and out towards the porch and the calf and said, "I know now where the father got the money to pay up the grocery bill with last week."

He had his arms folded, as was his custom, and as he walked up through the store and I followed him, he said, "Ben, I've got a milk-pen calf about that size and the cow is nearly dry and she's fat too. I'll sell you the cow and calf for $50 and whatever interest you've got in any other livestock in the community."

We went out to the barn close to the store to look at the cow and calf. The fat cow would bring probably $60 and the fat calf was worth more than the one I had lost, so we turned them into the road. I paid him the $50 and started driving my new stock back to town, and neither of us ever mentioned that Reddy Calf was the one that got away or that the calf he was givin' me, virtually speakin', had anything to do with money that he had got for the grocery bill.

COWBOY
BANKIN'

HOT JULY DAYS WILL CAUSE A COW-
boy to start long rides way before daylight so he can
shade up in the heat of the day and save his horse and
still get in a full day's ride. Shultz Bros. had leased the
Coleman pasture, about twelve miles north of Weatherford, and I was going out there to check around on the
cattle and come back that night or the next morning. I
had tied my horse to the telephone pole on the east side of
Huddleston's Drugstore, which was next door to the old
Texas Café. The old Texas Café was a landmark in
Weatherford that they had lost the key to. It had stood
open day and night to all comers for more than thirty
years. It was operated by Mr. Patrick and his son, Byron
Patrick, and twenty-four hours of the day one or the other
of them was there on duty. This was the meeting place for

everybody, whether they were leaving early or coming in late, and I had stopped by for an early breakfast. Little Pat had turned in my order for ham and eggs and hot biscuits. Nobody could ever have rightfully complained about the hospitality, the grub, or the atmosphere of the Texas Café. They had big stoves in the back corner and the front corner in the wintertime for their paying and nonpaying customers alike, and in the summertime there were big fans blowing outside from the kitchen and big fans blowing up in the front and ceiling fans swinging in the door and from the ceiling. It was the coolest place in town with a fifty-gallon barrel of ice water set on the counter with clean glasses for all comers. Many a businessman in town slipped out of bed early and didn't disturb his wife and came down to the Texas Café to get away from burned homemade toast and get hot biscuits for breakfast.

Fred Smith was the up-and-coming banker of the town that did lots of business with the cattlemen, traders, and farmers who were customers of the Citizens National Bank. He came in and sat down next to me and ordered hot cakes. Fred was a good banker and a good judge of cattle, but I told him right fast that whatever he was up early for wasn't going to take much hard work or he wouldn't be tanking up on them hot cakes. We had a lot of smart conversation during breakfast and when I was about to leave, I said, "Fred, I'm riding out early and won't be in town when the bank opens. (Bankers worked on Saturday just like everybody else in those days.) That note for $40 that I've got at the bank ain't due, but I've got the $40 in my pocket to pay it, and I've $160 in my pocket that I want you to deposit for me. I'll give you the money and you tend to it when you get to the bank."

Fred was my friend and even though I was a high-school kid he loaned me money on my signature just like I was a grown man. When I suggested that I give him this money out of my pocket and he put it in his pocket when it really belonged in the bank, he started in to give me a bringin'-up lecture on how to tend to my bank business.

He said, "Now Ben, you are a grown boy buying and selling horses and cattle and you're doing it in a grown-up, business-like manner and right now you just as well learn to do your banking business likewise. A bank is an institution that maintains a big headquarters with people to wait on you and money to loan you and a safe to keep all valuables, and what I'm trying to tell you is that anything that belongs to the bank, bring it or take it to the bank. I'm not going to be taking your deposits before daylight in the café or after dark down at the wagonyard or at the stock pens. You just as well learn now to bring it to the bank and do your banking business at the bank."

I looked across the counter at Little Pat and said, "Ain't he gettin' highfalutin. The next thing I know he'll be wantin' me to call him Mr. Smith." Pat just sort of chuckled and didn't get in on the conversation. As I got off the stool and started to leave, Fred started telling me that I shouldn't be giving my money to other people to do my banking for me and if I had ANYTHING THAT BE-LONGED TO THE BANK, BRING IT TO THE BANK.

It was still early and cool, and I rode to the Coleman pasture by the middle of the morning. After I had counted all the steers in the pasture and saw that there was plenty of salt in the trough and the windmill was running and there was plenty of water, I headed my horse on over to Springtown, which was only four or five miles. Late in the afternoon I rode back to the Coleman pasture, fed Beauty, and went to bed early on a saddle blanket spread out in tall sage grass.

I waked up before daylight, and it was a nice cool Sunday morning and I thought I would ride into town early. I started Beauty out at a nice flat walk to let her warm up slow and didn't intend to put a very hard ride on her since I had nothing to do that I knew of when I got to town. I topped the ridge about two miles north of town at Couch's barn. This was a big old rock barn that had been built by Mr. Couch, who was an early-day developer of the West, horse breeder, and founder of the Citizens National Bank. It had later been turned into a dairy barn.

Just as I topped the rise about even with the Couch barn, I heard an awful commotion, screamin', hollerin', and carryin' on over at the barn. A half-grown boy dived through the window about halfway up the barn wall and two screaming young girls came runnin' through the front door, followed by a grown man that was about to run over them. I could hear a lot of hollerin' and bawlin' and going on in the barn. I reined up my horse and rode over to the barn. It was barely daylight and I asked what the trouble was.

The reason there was so many hands out at the milk barn was that milking in those days was done by hand and it usually took a good-size family or several hired hands to run a dairy. It seemed they all got their breath at once and began to tell me about a bad fightin' cow had got in with their dairy cattle down in the pasture and that morning had horned her way into the barn to eat with the milk cows and when she realized there was people mixed up with the milk cows, this big yellow-brindle longhorn fat cow decided to clean the place out. The man spoke up to explain to me that the cow was one that had gotten away when a truckload of cattle had turned over on that hill a few days before.

I said, "Yeah, that's just another one of them cases that people are goin' to have to learn: cows or horses aren't made to haul in trucks. They get four or five of them in a big truck and they make it top-heavy, and comes around a curve or goin' down a hill it gets to swingin' and turns over. Cattle and horses weren't never intended to be hauled anyway. If the good Lord hadn't aimed for them to walk, he wouldn't have given them four feet and legs. Them trucks are all right, I guess, for corn, watermelons, or other stuff that can't move around."

While I was giving off my expert opinion on how to move stock, Mr. Dairyman spoke up and said that these cattle that were in the truck when it turned over belonged to the bank, and Fred Smith had told him when he got this one in a pen to call him and he would send me to get her. I told him that this was the first I had heard about this, but to have a bad cow fastened up in a barn would be taking advantage of her since I was used to having to catch them out in the brush, and I sure would be glad to get her now instead of having to come back after her when she was turned back out.

We were figuring on how to get in there and how to catch her, and I decided I didn't want to go in there on

horseback on that concrete floor to get my horse horned
and maybe slip down in as small a place as a dairy barn. I
had a hard, long maguey rope tied on my saddle, and I took
it in my hand and stepped inside the front door. They had
lights all over the barn and that old cow would run at a sha-
dow if it would move. She was standing in the middle of the
barn pawing like a bull, blowing her nostrils and shak-
ing her horns. I stood real still and watched her a minute.

The milk stanchions had been built out of two-by-four
and two-by-six lumber where the cows stuck their heads
through to eat while they were being milked. The plank
on one side of these old-fashioned milking stanchions
was solid. The other side had a bolt run through it at the
bottom and was swinging between the two-by-four
frames at the top, and after the cow had stuck her head
through the stanchion you pushed that one closed at the
top and latched it by swinging a little wood block against
it that was hinged on the other end. I decided that I
would go behind these stanchions against the wall, which
was about two feet of space, and let this old cow run at
me and when she got her head through I was going to
fasten the stanchion. Then I would have her caught and
that would give me plenty of time to put my rope on her.

Well, I got back behind the stanchion and it wasn't
any trouble to get her to run at me, but it took a lunge or
two for her to get her head turned to where her horns
would go through this milk-cow-size stanchion. When she
had her head just right, I reached over and pushed the
stanchion up and tripped the little block against it at the
top. After I had this done, the milk crew came in the front
door and Mr. Dairyman had gone around back to open

the back door when I said I was ready, and he had led ole Beauty around back for me to let her in when I had the cow ready to let out.

A maguey rope is hand-woven in Old Mexico out of long, fine, stout cactus fiber and each rope is woven and platted individually. The end of a maguey rope where it is started is smooth and does not have a knot like the end of a common rope that has been cut and tied, and the other end has a platted hondo that you slip the knot end through to form your loop.

I dropped my rope on this old cow's horns and she was bawlin' and lungin' and shakin' that row of stanchions with her 1,300 pounds that was well made out of two-by-fours and two-by-sixes, and at the rate that she was going I wasn't sure that she wasn't going to tear up the inside of the barn. I realized my fancy Mexican maguey wasn't stout enough to hold this 1,200- to 1,300-pound cow and that she was sure to charge my horse and cause a lot of trouble if I didn't outsmart her pretty fast.

There is not much you can do to hurt the outside of a mean, mad cow and whippin' and jerkin' would sort of be a joke. I put a half hitch around her nose and threw the rope over the top of the stanchion and lifted her head about two feet in the air; then I took my pocketknife and punched a hole in the fine cartilage between the two nostrils and about as far up as I could reach in her nose with my hand, sort of like you would put a ring in a bull's nose. I took the smooth end of the maguey rope and ran it into the cow's nostril and through the hole in the middle cartilage and then back down through the other nostril. I worked the rope back against her neck and towards her shoulder and out of the stanchion and hollered at Mr. Dairyman to open the door at the back and bring me my mare. He came in with his mouth open and his eyes about the size of goose eggs and handed me the reins from as far as he could stand.

These maguey ropes were about from forty-five to as much as sixty feet long and, to say the least, this was one of the longer ones. I got on my horse, took my rope, and dallied it around the saddle horn and ole Beauty snorted and looked at that concrete floor when I dallied it, which was as much as to tell me that she wouldn't have a chance to keep from slipping on that concrete. I told Mr. Dairyman to ease up behind the stanchion where I had been and when that old cow would stand still to trip the little block at the end of the stanchion, and I would be on my way out with her. His nerve failed him some and he picked up a stick about three feet long and used it to trip the little block and free the swinging side of the stanchion. That wild, mean, mad cow caught on fast. She thought she was loose and when she backed out of the stanchion Beauty and I dived through the back door of the barn and turned against the barn; as this cow ran out, she headed for the milk cows that had been turned out during the commotion. When I jerked the end of the rope and that little hard rope burned that hole in the inside of her nostril, she suddenly had a rude awakening—she was still caught—and while she was still giving to the pain to the rope in that hole in her nose, ole Beauty lunged back and turned her a flip. She got up off the ground facing us and made a wild lunge towards my horse. I had lots of slack in my rope. I flipped the slack over her neck as

Beauty dodged and jumped out of her way, and we busted her again. This time she got up and stood there quiverin' and shakin' and bawlin', and slobber and a little blood was running out of her nose and mouth. I was between her and the corral gate, so somebody opened the gate and she began to lead as I started outside with her. She made a wild run as we went through the gate, not at me and Beauty, but just to get away into the open. This time I didn't have to turn her, I just jiggled slack in that rope tied to her horns and through that hole in her nose and she began to take a little friendlier outlook on me and my horse's acquaintance.

I started down the road with her and when she would want to trot Beauty would move up enough to keep the slack out of the rope, and when she decided to slow down we would slow down with her, but I did keep my hold on the rope and jiggled it a little to keep her on notice that as far as she was concerned she was still caught by the end of her nose. I had by this time taken a double half hitch on my saddle horn with the rope so that I didn't have to hold it so tight. This gave me a loose hand to play with the slack in case she got smart.

I had gotten to the railroad tracks at the foot of the hill and was about to start up the hill to town when I wondered what I should do with this cow. I knew there was no use in trying to take her to the railroad stock pens because they would be locked. I thought Silas Kemp wouldn't care for me bringing a fightin' cow to the wagon-yard, and I knew I would have her at a place where I could get a lot of help to do whatever Fred Smith decided he wanted to do with her later. Just as I got to the corner of the wholesale-grocery warehouse where I would turn to go to the wagonyard, I had another bright, teen-age-cowboy Sunday idea about what to do with a mad fightin' cow that belonged to the bank. I led her on up the paved street early on Sunday morning with nobody in sight and rode around the telephone pole right in front of the bank door and made several wraps around the pole leaving the cow five or six feet of slack. I stepped off my mare and ran the rope around a concrete column at the bank door, then I threaded the end of the rope through the handle of the bank door and over to the concrete column on the other side of the door and tied the rope off to the last column.

I did all this in a matter of seconds and stepped on old Beauty and rode down to the telephone pole on the east side of the drugstore, tied my horse, and went to the Texas Café for breakfast. Little Pat waited on me and there were very few people around, and I was leisurely eatin' my breakfast when the phone rang and Pat answered it and I heard him say, "Yeah, he's here. You want him?" and then Pat hung up. As he walked back towards me he had a puzzled kind of look on his face and said, "Why is Fred Smith hunting you?" Looking as innocent as I could with a mouthful of ham and eggs, I blubbered and said I had no idea. As Pat started on to the kitchen, he said, "Fred said he would be down here in a few minutes."

Fred was a short, red-complexioned, nice-looking sort of a fellow whose black hair was getting thin on top and a little gray in the temples. All of a sudden he busted through that front door a-wearin' his house-shoes, a pair of regular britches, the top part of his pajamas, and no hat. When I looked up and saw him, before he had time to start on me, I said, "Fred, you must be confused. From the looks of your garb, you ain't decided whether you are gettin' up or goin' to bed."

"Don't be trying to start on my garb. That's not what I'm down here for. My phone's been ringing steady for the past ten minutes—people calling waking up the family telling me about a cow being tied to the bank door." In a mad kind of voice he said, "Ben, what cow is that and why in the hell did you tie her up in front of the bank?"

His remark didn't cause me to lose any interest in my breakfast, and between mouthfuls I explained to him where the cow came from.

By this time he was mad and nervous. Little Pat had set a cup of coffee out on the counter for him, but he didn't even sit down. He was walking up and down the aisle beating on the counter and talking to me.

"I'm glad you got her, but why didn't you take her to the wagonyard or to the stock pens or any place besides the public sidewalk in front of the bank?"

Little Pat was listening and by this time there were a few more people who had discovered the cow was tied to the bank door. I rared back and said, "Mr. Smith, ANYTHING THAT BELONGS TO THE BANK, TAKE IT TO THE BANK."

Pat blew coffee out of his mouth and took to the kitchen. Fred said, "Hell, I didn't mean a cow!"

By this time about everybody was laughing but Fred, and I wasn't going to laugh because I was being plumb innocent. I just told him that I was tryin' to learn the lesson that he was tryin' to teach me, and just yesterday mornin' he told me when I was tryin' to pay a note and give him some money to deposit, I said, "You told me

'ANYTHING THAT BELONGS TO THE BANK, TAKE IT TO THE BANK.' "

He finally broke into a little chuckle and said, "You've took her to the bank, now we've got to take her away from there before people start to Sunday school and church."

I said, "Fred, I am goin' to leave town in the mornin' before daylight to go to the Denton place below Brock to look at some horses and maybe buy them. Now if you was carryin' my money to pay the bank a note I owe for $40, and if you was goin' to deposit $160 of my money for me to check against to buy them horses with, then if you was goin' to put about $5 extra with it, we'll say for workin' stock, then I would need pretty bad to move that cow so you could get in the bank Monday mornin' to tend to mine and the bank's business."

He pounded his fat fist on the counter and said, "Hell, give me the money."

So I counted out $200 in tens and twenties and I said, in a humorous tone of voice, "Fred, when I work stock for people on Sunday, they usually buy my breakfast."

Pat busted out laughing again and said, "The breakfast is on the house."

I got my horse and went up and unwrapped this old cow from around the bank door and unwrapped her from the telephone pole and took her and put her in the wagon-yard. Fred got a hold of Ike Simmons, who was the porter at the barbershop, and they began to clean up that green splashy aftermath that comes from a mad cow. By church-time few people knew that the bank's cow business and my banking business had been tended to so early on Sunday morning.

PEDDY

I

WAS SETTIN' IN THE SADDLE SHOP
while Bill, the saddle maker, put some new riggin' in the
front of my saddle. I'd roped a big four-year-old wild mule

that morning; when I dallied the rope to the saddle horn, this big mule was stout enough that he tore the riggin' out of my saddle. I had managed to give him slack and at the same time wind him around a tree and tie him before we got in a storm and I lost my whole saddle. Bill was an old-time saddle maker and he never stopped talkin' while he worked, so I was hearin' stories about the times that other cowboys had tore their saddles up when in walked Mr. Davidson, who ran a dry-goods and furniture store next door. He had been to the post office and comin' back by came in to talk to me and Bill. He passed the time of day a few minutes talking about the weather and work and stuff. Then he turned to me and said, "Ben, I want to sell you eight two-year-old heifers worth the money."

I knew about his heifers, but I thought it might do him good to talk about 'em, so I didn't butt in. He said that he had a string of yearling steers in his pasture, and when he shipped 'em out in the spring the man that bought 'em didn't want these eight heifers that were in the bunch, so they had turned them back in the pasture.

He wanted to stock this pasture in the late fall with another bunch of steer yearlings and would like to get these heifers out of the way. I listened to all this and I liked Mr. Davidson; he was a nice kind of ole country merchant that ever'body some time or another had owed money to, and after thirty years in the community there still wasn't anybody that would say anything bad about Mr. Davidson. He took jokin' pretty good too. I knew that I'd make a trade with him before we quit talkin', but I felt like I ought to carry him on a little while, so after this explanation about his heifers I asked him how fat were they and how much would they weigh.

He said they were big fat, and would weigh about 600 pounds apiece.

I said, "Well, I guess they'd be worth about six cents a pound and that would be $36 a head; put them in the corral and I'll come get 'em."

He said, "Now, that's not quite the kind of a trade I want to make because these heifers'll bring about eight cents a pound, and you know I'm no cowboy and don't have anybody workin' for me to pen heifers, so why don't you just buy 'em and go gather 'em out of the pasture yourself?"

I said, "Mr. Davidson, I didn't know that you didn't like me."

He said, "Why Ben, what do you mean? You've always been one of my favorite boys."

I said, "Well, I know for a fact that Ole Slim Cartwright rode in that pasture at $3 a day until he paid his dry-goods bill and never did see hair nor hide of them heifers. And now you wanta sell 'em to me just like they'as a-standin' at the gate bawlin' to get out."

We had a big laugh and he admitted I was a-tellin' the truth.

I started out by tellin' him that it seemed to me like the circumstances would change the price of them heifers a whole lot and $36 apiece would be enough for 'em.

He started out then by tellin' me when I'd get the heifers out would have something to do with him sellin' 'em to me. This was early August, and I asked him how the fifteenth of September would suit him. He said that'd be early enough if my price was good enough.

I did some fast cowboy arithmetic in my head, and bid him $225 for the bunch. He hemmed and hawed around and looked at the mail that he had in his hand and 'lowed as how he ought to get $250 for 'em. That little remark as much as told me that I already had 'em bought.

So after a little more jaw work he took me up and I paid him for the heifers.

The weather was hot and I rode this pasture from daylight until about noon and then from about three o'clock in the afternoon till dark for five straight days without findin' the heifers. This bunch of heifers hadn't been run and they weren't spoiled or outlawed; they were just by instinct wild, and too, the grazing was better in the thickets and valleys than it was out of the open mesas. The summer foliage was extremely dense, and standin' out on the bluffs horseback tryin' to spot brownish-red and brindle cattle in a thicket below was not easy.

This particular afternoon I had ridden up on a high mesa that had a steep bluff lookin' off to the east. The fence line ran so close under the bluff that you couldn't see it from a standin' position on top of the mesa. The mesa overlooked a small farm to the east that faced out on a country road at the other side of it. As I sat there on my horse wonderin' where else to look for my heifers, I saw little Peddy ridin' Queenie comin' up across the field.

Queenie was a small grey mare of mine that was about sixteen years old. She had taught half of the town kids how to ride horseback, and the fall before this I had taken her away from some kids in town that were runnin' her up and down the streets and not takin' very good care of her. She was gonna bring a colt in the spring, and I had started to the pasture that I had leased down the road in front of Peddy's house.

When Peddy came out to the road, as he often did when I passed, and stretched his hands up to me to pick him up and carry him in front of me on my horse. This time I had reached over from my saddle and picked Peddy up and set him on Queenie that I was leadin', and let him ride her back to his house.

Peddy had had a very serious sickness when he was only three or four years old and had always been frail and had lots of sick spells. He was a good little boy, but his older brothers and sisters never had bothered to play with him and his mother and daddy didn't have much time to spend with him.

Peddy laid around on the porch in the summertime and in front of the fire in the wintertime, and had taken very little exercise. His mother, Amy, had never been able to get him to eat very much.

When we got to the house, he didn't want to get off of Queenie. He didn't make any fuss, nor cry, but he got around to askin' me if Queenie could stay at his house a few days. Peddy couldn't talk plain and his voice was weak, but his big eyes put forth a very convincing argument, and I had left Queenie there almost a year ago. Queenie had kept Peddy out in the sunshine and fresh air, and caused him to take exercise and he was growin' into a healthy, chuffy little boy. Queenie had brought a colt in the spring, and it was nearly grown and was fol-lowin' as he rode across the fields.

I had watched him a few minutes when he looked up and saw me up on the bluff. He waved real big with his ragged straw hat for me to meet him at the north corner of the field. I rode down to the fence line as Peddy rode up, and in his broken dialect he asked me to crawl over the fence and we'd eat a watermelon. That sounded like a good proposition to me. We walked out among the watermelon vines and Peddy picked out one that looked a little overripe, and when I suggested that we get a differ-ent one, he said, he'd give this one first to Queenie and then we could have a better one.

We got a good melon and got under the shade of a tree on the fence line of the pasture. Peddy asked me what I was doin' in the Davidson pasture, and I told him about buyin' the heifers and that I was lookin' for 'em. Peddy was a serious little boy; I suppose because he had been sick so much in his life. He didn't hoorah and play much, and he seemed to have wisdom far beyond his years concerning pets and dumb animals. As we ate the watermelon I told him that I'ad put out some feed for the heifers, but they had never been fed and probably wouldn't come to feed.

Peddy had pulled some salt, wrapped up in wax paper, out of the pocket of his homemade shirt that we had been usin' on the watermelon. He held the salt up in his hand and said, "Ben, hepers like sol."

I said, "Peddy, I know heifers like salt, but if I put a sack o' salt out in the pasture, they'd eat as much as they wanted in a few days, and I might not get a chance to drive 'em out when they came to salt."

Peddy looked very serious and said, "Don't put out no sack, hepers lick sol outa yer han."

I didn't laugh at Peddy unless he said something that he knew was funny because Peddy had been laughed at too much by people because he couldn't talk. I studied about what Peddy had said as I flipped watermelon seeds off of the piece I was about to eat.

I said, "Peddy, gentle heifers would lick salt out of your hand, but these heifers are wild."

Peddy looked over the fence to the other side at Queenie as though he was tryin' to figure out a way to make me understand. He held the salt up again in the paper and said, "Hepers lick sol out of Peddy's han. They no wil. I sol hepers when I sol Queenie when she under tree."

This was the only shade tree in the field and when Queenie was in the field loose Peddy would bring salt to catch Queenie with, and he said that he had been lettin' the heifers lick salt out of his hand through the fence.

This sounded too good to be true! But Peddy was a good little boy and was not jokin' about the heifers lickin' out of his hand, and he convinced me of it in broken sentences and the serious look on his face.

We were about finished with the watermelon, and I said, "Peddy, what's Queenie's colt's name?"

He said, "Queenie hav' Princ, what do you think?" and then smiled real big.

I told Peddy that I would take the fence down, and

the next time the heifers came to the fence he could give 'em some salt and after they were out in the field I'd put the fence back up.

Peddy said that these heifers came to that thicket under the bluff by the tree about every third day. I pondered this and knew that that would be so true because cattle range over a big pasture, and make it back to certain spots at intervals. It was evident that Peddy had watched for 'em and fed 'em salt out of his hand and knew what he was talkin' about.

He said that "they'd no be there tomorro', but would be there the nex' day," which I knew would be Friday.

I asked Peddy why he didn't have a saddle on Queenie. He told me it hurt her sides when he tightened it up, and he didn't mind ridin' bareback. He got a hold of Queenie's mane and crawled up her foreleg with his bare toes as I crawled over the fence and got on my horse, and we waved at each other and rode away.

I studied about the heifers having been in the pasture all summer without any salt. Hot weather and green pasture cause cattle to crave salt, and when they smelled Queenie licking from Peddy's hand, they came to the smell by instinct.

The next day I took a ten-pound sack of table salt and tied it on my saddle and rode out to Peddy's house. Ace, his father, was home and I told him about mine and Peddy's conversation and watermelon eatin' the day before. His mother was listenin' and she broke out laughin' and said that she had wondered what Peddy had been doin' with all the table salt.

Peddy came in while we were talkin' and we discussed

our plans about the heifers. Ace and Amy went on at
length about how much good Queenie had done for
Peddy and now he was strong enough to start to school
this fall, which would be his first year. They talked on
about Peddy feeding Queenie before he would eat breakfast, dinner, or supper.

Ace said that he'd go up to the back of the field and let
the fence down. Peddy broke in to warn us that the
"hepers were no fra'd of Peddy, but mit be afra'd of big
mans." So we agreed to let him try it his own way.

The next day Peddy was up at sunup and went to the
watermelon patch on Queenie and sure 'nuff, the heifers
worked their way up to the fence. I was settin' up on top
of the bluff, horseback, when I watched eight two-year-
old heifers follow a small boy and a little ole grey mare
out from under the bluff and down into an open field. I
came off the bluff and put up the fence behind him.
Peddy walked on the ground and the heifers one at a time
would follow along and lick salt out of his hand. Ace
came out away around and away from the heifers and
Peddy. I came up from behind and neither of us did anything to help or made a sound, while Peddy and Queenie
tolled eight fat, brownish-red crossbred heifers into a
corral.

Ace shut the gate, with Peddy tellin' him not to
"kare" 'em. I rode up and got down off of my horse.
Peddy wasn't anxious to get out of the lot and he poured
a little more salt out of the sack into a trough as he led
Queenie toward the corral gate. Ace opened the gate and
let him out.

Of course, I was all smiles and I'as a-braggin' on

Peddy and a-braggin' on Queenie, and for the first time since I had known Peddy, he literally beamed over what he had done!

This was the best heifer-gatherin' that I had ever had. I had bought 'em awful cheap; they were bigger'n either Mr. Davidson or I had guessed 'em and sure 'nuff would bring eight cents a pound.

I said, "Peddy, I'm gonna put you in the cow business. Pick out the heifer you want, and I'll give 'er to you."

Peddy looked at me and looked at Ace and got very serious, and in a broken, stammerin' voice, said he'd ruther have Queenie. I told Peddy that the heifer would make him the most money.

He buried his face in Queenie's mane and rubbed her neck with his hands and said, "Queenie make me well."

I looked at Ace and he was tryin' to get something out of his eye.

I couldn't think of any reason to want Queenie, so I cleared my throat, and in a clear, firm voice said, "Peddy, get on *your* mare and help me up the road with these heifers."

SCOTCH
HIGHLAND
CATTLE IN THE
ROCKIES

A KANSAS CITY BANK SPECIALIZES
in cattle loans over much of the western part of the United States. I had worked for them in the Southwest in several different cow deals, and this is how I got into this wild cow deal in the Rocky Mountains.

A Scotsman by the name of Scotty Perth had long been a customer of the bank. His ranch was on the western slope of the Rockies and between bad winters and dry summers and other personal financial disasters, Scotty's business had gotten in bad shape. He was asking the bank for another advance when they got into some misunderstanding and in an outburst of his Scotch-Irish temper, he bluffed the bank into taking his cattle, range delivery, and mark all his notes "Paid." He still owned the ranch that the cattle were on, and the bank had until the first of January to have the cattle rounded up and moved off of Scotty Perth's land.

I had taken the contract to gather three hundred head of cattle (the mortgage called for three hundred head and their increase) that were crossbred between Longhorn Scotch Highland cattle and good Hereford cattle. This is the reason that I was suddenly transplanted from the far, hot Southwest to the high, cool regions of the Rocky Mountains. ·

I had shipped ten head of horses from Texas and had been on the ranch that was known as Scotty's Canyon for about a week. During that week I realized how much trouble I was in! Scotty's Canyon only had one partition fence on the whole ranch, which meant that there were two great big pastures. When Scotty Perth traded with the bank and got his notes marked paid, he specified that they were not to use his headquarters, corrals, and trap pastures to hold cattle in during the time they were being rounded up for shipment. This meant that the only other corrals were high up in the canyon in a very bad spot to try to corral cattle.

This corral high up in the mountains was in the head of a box canyon where a high shaft of rock was at the back of the canyon against the mountain, and the mountain was steep on both sides and at the lower end, which was about three hundred yards from the back, there was a crude rock fence about five to six feet tall that had been built by hand. It was spread out wide on the bottom on the outside of the fence and the rock had been laid reasonably straight up and down on the inside of the corral. This corral was an ancient landmark and was referred to by the natives as the Indian Horse Corral. The story went that Indians had built it to trap wild horses in and no one seemed to know how long it had been there. There was an opening but no swinging gate, and poles had to be fixed across it when stock had been penned. Over to the east of this Indian Corral and up about three hundred yards above there was a mountain not nearly as high as the rest of the mountain range that surrounded it. This little mountain had a trail winding up to the top of it, and it was a mesa of about four or five acres covered with flat rock. This landmark was known as Teepee Rock.

I had made my camp on top of Teepee Rock and was keeping my saddle horses in the Indian Rock Corral at night until I got them located and trained to come in to feed. There was a dripping spring about a hundred yards down the trail off of Teepee Rock and I cleaned out a little basin for it to settle in, and this is where I got water for my camp and to drink.

The location of this corral was bad and something else still worse than this was the fact that my good, hard Texas cow horses were at about a three-thousand-foot-higher elevation and were out of wind after a short ride in that high mountain country, which meant that I didn't have enough speed in my horses to outrun cattle that were native at this altitude.

I had ridden out Scotty's Canyon from one end to the other and was gettin' ready to make my first big drive. I hired three native cowboys that agreed to mount themselves on their own horses for $5 a day apiece. This was about $2 a day higher than the wages in the rest of the country, but it seemed that most people were in sympathy with Scotty Perth, or else did not want to cultivate his dislike by helpin' gather the cattle that he had by now begun to take the attitude and spread the word that the bank was "takin'" away from him.

The first day's ride was a pretty wild one, but since we had lots of cattle in front of us and they hadn't been choused, we netted one hundred and twenty-three head that day. After we got 'em in the canyon corrals we had to drive 'em back down into the pastures and into the valley and by Scotty's headquarters before we got 'em out into the open country to start 'em to the railroad. I couldn't help but wonder if we'd spill a bunch of 'em the next day goin' back down through the pasture.

We sat around camp that night and spun a few yarns, and I listened to some of the local wild cow tales before we went to bed.

Next morning we had breakfast and had ridden to the top of the canyon and were ready to turn the cattle out by daylight. It was light enough that you could see a cow and tell her from a boulder or a bush when I gave the signal to start the cattle out of the corrals. I rode the point and had a man on each wing and the older and slower cowboy that I had hired to bring up the drags. We made it fine through the first pasture, and we were almost through the gate with the herd when the old cowboy bringin' up the drags "accidentally" let about twenty head get away, but we couldn't stop and make a drive for them so we started on down the canyon with what we had. The cattle bawlin' and runnin' down the canyon gave us a pretty wild ride, but while they were doin' it, they attracted the attention of a lot of the cattle that were in this pasture that hadn't been run the day before. So wild cattle like that began to run into and gather with the herd we were drivin'. Once, glancing over my shoulder, I saw the man ridin' wing to the left almost tryin' to keep some cattle from comin' into the herd. This aroused my curiosity and immediately I began to wonder if these native cowboys were tryin' to help me or maybe they were still tryin' to help Scotty Perth.

We were gettin' to the end of the pasture, about an hour and a half later, and the cattle had settled down pretty good and didn't appear to be mindin' the drive too much. Since I was ridin' point, I broke out ahead pretty fast and opened the big double gates that led out into the road. As I mounted my horse and turned back towards the herd, I noticed another one of my good cowboys droppin' back like he intended to let the point of the herd turn back and start a run into the flat rock at the foot of the mountains. I squalled at him real loud and rode back hard to straighten up the point of the herd. When the herd started through the gate I glanced around and all three of my cowboys were more than a half mile back on the side of the mountain settin' in a little huddle and the cattle were followin' each other and bawlin' and comin' on through the gate without any help drivin' 'em from behind. This was all the proof I needed that I had a roadful of cattle started to the railroad twenty miles away without too much help!

Directly they broke into a lope and caught up and hollered a few times and played like they was really busy, but the truth of the matter was these extra cattle that joined us in the second pasture was quite a surprise to 'em, and the drive was going to be far more successful than their original plans. It was a nice, cool mountain summer day. The cattle were fat and drifted along on the trail without much trouble and were coverin' the distance to town better than any cowboy could have hoped that they would trail.

We didn't have any grub with us, and we had made the day without any dinner, but by three thirty in the afternoon I counted one hundred and forty-seven head of cattle through the gate and into the railroad shippin' pens. I pulled the chain around the gate and locked it with the railroad lock and breathed a sign of relief. We had all acted pleasant all day, and I hadn't gotten after anybody about their bad way of handlin' cattle, so I told these native cowboys that I'd go by the depot and order some stockcars to ship in and then I'd meet them uptown in the dining room of the local hotel and we'd eat.

We had a pretty silent kind of a dinner, for cowboys, and I didn't notice too many of the natives tryin' to be friendly with my help.

These fellows had hired out to me and brought out their bedrolls and their extra horses and durin' dinner they'd told me that they was gonna stay with me till I got those cows if "it took all winter." Well, that might have been their plans, but I had a different idea about it.

We spent the night in town, and by dark all three of 'em disappeared from the hotel and they didn't show up at the stock pens until up in the middle of the mornin' to start back to the ranch. I was real friendly and let on like the late start was all right—that I kinda wanted to loaf around a little bit that morning and get acquainted with the town and it wouldn't hurt if the other cattle had a day to settle in the canyon anyway.

We rode into camp about one o'clock, and all of us set about to stir up some dinner. We'd cooked up a batch of stuff and pretty well devoured it by about two o'clock. And the old cowboy that had let some cattle get away the first chance he had had brought up the matter of whether we oughta ride that afternoon or not. I pulled out my checkbook and said, "Yeah, I think so. But I intend for it to be back to town for you would-be cowboys because I can let these cattle get away without any help and, more'n that, if some wild cattle come and try to get in the herd, I don't need anybody to fight 'em back, and if some want to go through a gate, I don't need a cowboy to scare 'em back, and so far as I can tell that's the only system that you'all intend to use."

They stood real quiet and still while I made out their checks; then they went to gatherin' up their bedrolls and catchin' their extra horses and doin' a considerable amount of mouthin' between themselves about getting fired and makin' some pretty rash statements about Texas cowboys.

None of this bothered me too much as I had eased over by my bedroll where my extra clothes and saddle and grub were stacked and I'ad sat down on the ground and slipped my arm up in under a sack of flour and casually laid my little fist on the handle of a .45 pistol that I didn't intend to ever pull out as long as things didn't get beyond cussin' and conversation stage.

And sure 'nuff they rode off carrying their belongin's, their horses, and their ill-will with them!

This left me with one hundred and fifty-three wild cattle in two big rough pastures without any help.

The next day I tidied up my camp a little bit and rode into town to see if I had any mail. I had been into the post office and told 'em who I was and what I was doin' there and to hold any mail for me . . . that I'd come in occasionally to pick it up. I had a few letters of no particular importance.

The post office was in the mercantile as was most everything else in the town, includin' the loafers and the other local talent, such as advisers, wore-out cowboys, and even a few nice people. I tore one of these letters open and was standin' by the doorway readin' it when the village doctor, whom I had met, glanced up and said, "Ben, that letter must be good news."

I said, "Yes, it's from an old friend by the name of Russell Graham that's got a horse and mule deal that he's workin' on for me and him this winter."

The doctor stopped cold in his tracks and dropped his

jaw down and said, "Russell Graham! The name sounds familiar."

I said, "I don't guess you know him . . . he was raised out west of Fort Worth a little piece."

The old doctor turned all smiles and said, "I guess I would. He had an older brother about my age named Harve. We moved from that country when I was in high school."

This was the beginning of a pleasant visit and a valuable friendship, and we spent half the afternoon talkin' about old times.

He asked about many people that I could tell him all about, and he seemed to enjoy our conversation. By this time he suggested it was a long way back to Scotty's Canyon and that I must put my horse in his barn and spend the night.

The doctor had a nice family and home, and while I took on a dose of this hospitality I gathered much information about Scotty Perth, whom I had never seen, and the cow deal.

Scotty Perth was a Scotch-Irish orphan who came to America when he was sixteen years old with a herd of cattle for a Scotch land syndicate that was establishing a ranch in the Rocky Mountains. He was a big, hard Scotsman that had made the most of his opportunities and through hard work and honesty had acquired the ranch known as Scotty's Canyon. He had a large family and had built a home in town when they started coming of school age, and Scotty spend much of his time at the ranch alone in recent years, until a horse had fallen down a canyon wall with him and broke his left leg. He had lain out in the pasture a day and a night and by his toughness had managed to crawl and drag himself to his headquarters. It was still another day or two until anybody came by to find him. The final results of this was that Scotty lost his left leg . . . it had to be taken off. And it was durin' this spell that his financial difficulties had occurred and that he had developed an unbearable temper and in a fit of rage had settled with the bank by giving them all his cattle, range delivery. However, he still owned all of his ranch land and his friends hoped that he would be able to start over when the bank finally got the cattle moved off the ranch.

I rode out early next mornin' after I had thanked the good doctor and his wife for a most enjoyable visit. I knew that I could catch some more cattle by myself, but I didn't know how many. And it seemed that there weren't any cowboys that were gonna be willin' to help gather these cattle under the circumstances.

I rode and worked hard by myself for the next two weeks and got thirty-two head, which was about a carload of cattle.

By now I had learned something about runnin' wild cattle in the Rockies that was just reverse from runnin' wild cattle in the Southwest. In the Southwest cattle are usually in creek and river bottoms and around canyon pastures. The problem, generally speakin', is to bring them out and up into open prairie regions where they can be caught or driven. Now in the Rockies wild cattle take to the high country where the boulders and cliffs make it almost impossible to run a horse, and the problem is to get them down out of the mountains into the valleys below, which are usually open, and makes it possible to drive or herd or do whatever else you need to do with them.

My horses had begun to get acclimated to the high, light atmosphere, and the cattle had gotten wiser and wilder by the day—as the numbers dwindle, the work gets rougher in bad cow country.

I managed to get a couple of high-school boys to come out on Saturday and help me drive the carload I had gathered to the railroad. They were good kids, but it was the early fall and they had started to school and I wasn't gonna be able to run my business with just a little Saturday help.

In all the cattle that I had gathered there hadn't been one single pure-blooded Longhorn Scotch Highland cow. However, I had seen a few of them, but they were always at the front of the ones that were gettin' away. They were a shaggy, brownish-red breed of cattle of medium size and were not the best beef cattle in the world; but due to their native Scottish breeding and their long hair they were good cattle for the bitter winters of the Rocky Mountains. The crossbreeds raised from Hereford and Durham crosses were wonderful cattle with lots of extra stamina gained from the cross with better beef qualities coming from the other side of the cross. The crossbreeds had more red in their color and were splashed about the head and neck and underbellies with white. All of them had a lot longer, higher-pointed horns than Herefords or Durhams, but nothing to compare with some of the Mexican-Texas cattle I had handled.

I began to set snares and push rocks around to stop up

trails and had resorted to ropin' and draggin' one cow at a time, which got into hard work for me and my horses and in the long run gathered a very few cattle. I followed this kind of practice for about a month and there were still a lot more than a hundred cattle left in Scotty's Canyon.

Dr. Turner and I were settin' in front of the mercantile on a bench whilin' away the time one afternoon when a big, past-middle-age man with one peg leg started across the street.

As I watched his approach, I looked at the doctor, who must have known what I was thinkin' and said, "Yep, that's him."

Scotty was over six feet tall. His entire body was well proportioned and in spite of a peg leg and his age, he still moved with grace—and there was an unmistakable pride in his carriage. It could well be said that he was a handsome man. He had an abundance of sandy hair and beard and medium-blue eyes wide set in a large face that was in keepin' with his broad shoulders and body. However, the small lines of bitterness that had begun to form at the corners of his mouth and up through the middle of his chin were not appropriate on his handsome, expressive Scotch-Irish face.

I said a low tone of voice, "I'd like to meet him."

When he got nearly even with us the doctor raised up and said, "Scotty, I want you to meet Ben Green from Texas."

Scotty already knew who I was because as his home was on the road at the edge of town he had seen me drivin' his cattle to the stock pens. I had stood up straight and extended my hand, but he turned on his peg leg and did not offer to shake hands.

Instead he broke loose in his Scottish brogue and clipped his words hard and sharp and said, "I choose not to be friendly with the 'hireling' of a bank that would take a 'Kattleman's' herd from his land—and to make it worse they send this slight lad from Texas mounted on ponies to do the riding of a man and horses. Then an old and trusted friend and the doctor that has tended to the needs of me and my family would call him 'friend' and heap more insult on Scotty Perth by suggesting that I make his acquaintance."

With this blast at me off his chest, he turned and moved off so smoothly that I almost forgot he had a peg leg.

There were several people standing in earshot that began to turn and ease away. I was embarrassed to silence and the doctor started to apologize for Scotty and in a way was defending him.

I turned and started to the hitch rack to mount my horse and said in a whipped tone of voice, "I guess I would be better off out in the mountains."

Dr. Turner said, "I'll be looking for you back in town in a few days."

His tone was friendly and kind. I said, "Thank you, I'm glad there is one Texan lives here," as I stepped on my horse and rode out of town. Scotty Perth had embarrassed me before the doctor and the others listening, but the worst thing he done to me was that he had made some belittling remarks about the best band of horses that I had ever owned when he insinuated that "Texas ponies" (as he put it) were not good horses. Second, I didn't appreciate the tone of his voice or the look on his face when he referred to me as a "slight lad."

I stayed in my camp and rode after cattle for about two weeks during which time nobody came around my camp, which was about seven miles off the public road. I had begun to understand even better why nobody found Scotty Perth when he broke his leg. Every day I rode the pasture hazing the cattle out of the high pasture into the pasture that sloped to the valley; finally I knew that I had all the cattle out of the high pasture. I was sure that there were a lot more cattle left in Scotty's Canyon than it would take to make my total count of three hundred, including the cattle that I had already shipped. Three hundred was the number the bank had talked about.

In making the trade with the bank to gather the cattle, we had agreed that I was to be paid $3 a head to gather three hundred head, and that I was to gather all the rest of the cattle on the ranch for $1 a head. In the trade the bank was to pay me for gathering the first hundred and fifty head when I shipped them. And I had agreed to not draw any more money until all the cattle had been rounded up and taken off Scotty Perth's ranch. This was the bank's way of bein' sure that the ranch would be clean of all cattle. The only part of the contract that was in my favor was that the bank had paid for shippin' my horses from Texas and had agreed that when the job was finished they would pay for shippin' my horses back to Texas.

The nights had begun to get cold and Indian summer had past, meaning that I was ridin' against weather as well as time because when winter set in I wouldn't be able to ride and accomplish very much in deep snow. This meant that I had to gather the cattle in a much shorter time than the contract between the bank and Scotty Perth specified, which was the first of January.

It was time for me to make a trip into town to get some horseshoes, grub, and some feed for my horses. On these trips I would take three pack horses and tie each one's halter rope to the next one's tail and lead 'em single file behind my saddle horse. I'd pack these three horses with two hundred-pound sacks of oats, swingin' one each side to the packsaddle. This would be about almost twenty bushels that I'd take back to my camp to feed my saddle horses.

I rode in behind the country mercantile and tied my saddle horse and untied the pack horses from each other and let them drag their halter ropes and graze on the vacant land behind the mercantile until I was ready to load them. It was early afternoon when I got to town and I went about buyin' my list of supplies, and when I came to horseshoes and horseshoe nails, Dr. Turner had walked into the store and said to me, "I see you are buying some horseshoes. I noticed the horse you left in my stable one night had a good overreach when he walked. One of my horses travels that way, but I can't get him shod to where he won't forge and strike the heels of his front feet with the toes of his back feet."

I was glad to show off a little as the doctor was the only friend I had in town, so I told him I'd be glad to shoe his horse where it wouldn't forge.

I gave my list to the clerk at the mercantile to fill and

got in a model-T Ford with Dr. Turner and went down to his barn. He had plenty of horseshoeing tools and his horse was real gentle. Some of his kids rode the horse, and he kept him to drive in the winter when the roads were too bad to make calls in his model-T.

He sat in the doorway of the saddle room while I dressed his horse's feet and shod him. We led the horse around the corral after he was shod and one of the doctor's little girls rode him enough that Dr. Turner was convinced I'd shod him properly and that his front and back feet weren't goin' to interfere.

We were visitin' while the girl rode the horse, and he said, "If you are not in too big a hurry I've another horse in Town Trap [Town Trap was the little pasture down on the creek that nearly ever'body used to keep town horses in] that I wish you would shoe for me."

I told him I was sure I had enough time if it wouldn't take too long to catch the horse. His daughter spoke up and said it wouldn't be any trouble to catch the horse. She got a little feed out of the barn in a sack and an extra catch rope and jumped on the horse bareback and said she'd be back in a little while. In the meantime her daddy had been tellin' her which horse to catch.

We went to the house and Dr. Turner's wife fixed us some cake and coffee, and I took on a little hospitality while we were waitin' on the girl to bring the horse back. The conversation was light; he hadn't mentioned Scotty Perth and neither had I. The little girl was back in a few minutes and I went out to the barn to shoe the horse.

As we left the house, Mrs. Turner insisted that I come to town to church next Sunday. The church had a new preacher who was coming to preach every other Sunday, and she was havin' a church party after the meetin' for him this comin' Sunday and for me to be sure to come.

Both the horses were big bays of mixed blood, and you could tell that they were bound to be kinfolks. I said somethin' about how much they were alike, and Dr. Turner told me the horses were full brothers. I shod this horse very much like the first one, and sure 'nuff he traveled good too.

This must have taken about an hour and a half, and it was gettin' along past middle afternoon, so we went back to town and I finished gettin' groceries and horse feed tied on to my pack horses while Dr. Turner stood around and visited with me. A few people went in and out the back door of the mercantile. Most of 'em spoke to the doctor, but none of 'em bothered to nod or even notice that I was there. I couldn't quite get used to this kind of treatment. I was by nature loud-mouthed and friendly with ever'body, but the whole town seemed to resent me because I was roundin' up Scotty Perth's cattle for the bank.

I rode out of town rather late and put my pack horses in front of me so I could drive 'em a little faster than they'd normally lead in order to get back to my camp before night. I stayed around camp the next day, shod my saddle horses, did a little more extra cookin' than common. The weather was sort of cloudy and disagreeable, and I didn't try to work any cattle that day.

The next mornin' I saddled a horse called Charlie that was a nice saddle horse and good to make wild cattle runs on, but he was not too trustworthy a horse to rope from. I rode out on the side of the mountain and looked through the valley as I had done a number of times and sat there and gazed at Scotty Perth's headquarters with all its big corrals and barns that he had refused to let anybody use to hold cattle while they were workin' the canyon pastures.

I noticed a small bunch of cattle graze out into a clearin' at the foot of the mountain. I'd tried lots of times to push little bunches of cattle down into the valley and out at the gate by myself. These cattle were so wild and the rocks so rough and slick under your horse that it seemed impossible for one man to ever get any number of cattle through the gate and out into the road. An extra bull grazed out from the timber and joined this bunch of cattle and the bull that was with them started a fight.

For the moment I forgot I was ridin' Charlie who wasn't a good ropin' horse and I hurried down the mountain and charged these fightin' cattle before they had time to realize I was there. I roped a big crossbred brownish-red bull; judgin' from the length and size of his horns he must have been about five years old. Charlie didn't get too excited, and I managed to drag and jerk the bull around while the other cattle bawled and ran off.

Then it dawned on me that wild cattle, the climate, and the anger of Scotty Perth must be affecting my judgment. What was I gonna do with one big bull on the end of a lariat rope? Situations like this cause you to make up your mind pretty fast.

He charged my horse a time or two, and I managed to rein Charlie out of the way and whirl him and stop the bull. Durin' this wild bull play, the bull ran around a good-size tree, with the lariat rope wrapped around the tree, which took the strain off of Charlie and stopped the bull from being able to run back at us.

When you're not doin' much of your own thinkin', it's nice to get a wild bull to help you out. I had him roped around the horns, and there was no danger of him choking, so I untied the lariat from my saddle horn and jumped off my horse and tied the other end of the rope to another tree that was about the right distance from the tree he was wrapped to. This got Charlie and me away from the bull, but he was still a long ways from the railroad stock pens.

I stood on the ground beside my horse and looked at the bull and decided that I ought to tie him to somethin' light enough that he could drag, but heavy enough that he couldn't run away with it. I knew where there was some dead logs up the canyon a piece that I had been jumpin' my horse over. Any good cowboy that thinks he's goin' to get in trouble has more than one rope, so I rode up there and picked out a log that I thought was about the right size and tied on to it and drug it with my horse back down close to the bull.

The log was just about all a good saddle horse could drag to the saddle horn. By this time this mountain bull was sure mad. He had already pawed a good-size hole around the bottom of the tree, but he hadn't learned to turn and go the other way, which would've gotten him unwound from the first tree. I untied the rope from around the tree, keepin' an eye on the bull, afraid he might untangle himself before I got ready for him to. I worked the end of the lariat rope under this big log and tied it between two knots on the log where I knew it wouldn't slip off or come undone.

I got back on my horse, took my other rope, and rode up to the bull and whipped him around with the other rope and drove him around the right direction of the tree about three times. When he thought he was loose he made a wild run at my horse, and when the slack took up between him and the log it was quite a shock to him. It was some satisfaction to me to think maybe I was smarter than the bull.

This took a long time, and it was way past dinnertime. So I rode away and left the bull in a valley tied to a log and thought I would see what happened by tomorrow mornin'.

After I ate a little late dinner, I changed horses and rode back to see about my bull. He had drug that log down into the valley and almost to Scotty Perth's headquarters fence. As it was gettin' late in the afternoon I didn't go close to him I turned and went back to the camp for the night.

The moon came up about three or four o'clock in the mornin' and bawlin' cattle waked me. A cowboy layin' out in camp durin' the night handlin' wild cattle or bad horses don't take off too many clothes when he goes to bed in cold weather. All I had to do was pull on my boots, buckle my belt, and reach for my jacket and hat and I was what some people would have called dressed.

I saddled a horse called Mustang. He had no mustang blood in him, but he was one of the best horses that ever lived if you were in a tight with wild cattle or needed a good horse under you for any kind of a hard ride. When I came in sight of the valley, it was still a little while to daylight, but it was a bright night and I could see what was goin' on.

This mad, bawlin' bull had called his bunch of cows back to him, and the other bull that he was havin' the fight with when I caught him. I couldn't quite count the exact number but I knew there would be enough for a carload. I rode quiet and circled wide to the big double gates on the road. I opened them back and tied them to the fence where there would be no danger of them blowin' to in case a wind came up.

Today's modern cowboys probably don't know this, but cattle will drive better in bright moonlight than they will in the daytime because their vision at a distance lacks a little bit bein' good enough to judge a rider's position. And as long as they are movin' from you and you don't try to head 'em, they'll bunch and drive together good.

I circled around and came up on the east side of 'em. The gate was on the west. I didn't make too much wild cowboy noises. I carried a bull whip tied on my saddle for just such occasions as this. I uncoiled the whip and cracked it in dull tones in the still night air. This was a noise that these cattle didn't quite know about, and I stayed far enough away from 'em that they were movin' west little by little as the two bulls fought and about as fast as the bull could drag his log.

Just before sunup I had them bunched in a corner of the fence right in front of the double gate. As they began to drift out into the road without seemin' to know it, I counted thirty-seven head. I shut the gates and had my cattle in the road, but I had to untie that bull from the log if I was goin' to drive him with the herd of cattle twenty miles to town.

These cattle milled around in the road, and it was gettin' good daylight. I got off my horse and eased up the side of the road fence where my log-draggin' bull had stopped. He was on the other end of a forty-foot lariat rope and was pretty well worn out from draggin' the log and bein' horned by a bull that he couldn't very well defend himself against. I crawled under the fence and eased up toward the log, feelin' that the fence would give me a little protection. I laid down on my belly on the ground and wiggled through far enough on the back side of the log, took my pocketknife, and cut the rope.

I scooted back under the fence, walked back down to where my horse was, got back out in the road, and got on my horse, and started a cow drive to town with thirty-seven head of wild cattle. This was the best stunt I had pulled in several weeks and I was really proud of myself.

The drive to town was kinda easy. This was a mixed bunch of cattle, all ages and sizes—and there was a mahogany-brown long-haired one that I believed to be a pure-blooded Scotch Highland cow. I had heard it said that these pure-blooded cows were probably twenty years old if any of 'em were still alive. (It had been about that long since Scotty Perth had imported them.) This cow looked to be that old; however, she apparently had not had a calf in recent years and was in good flesh and led the herd to town.

The railroad stock pens were at the edge of town and not too hard to get to from the road that I had brought these cattle on. It was late afternoon when me and Mustang pushed this bunch of cows into the railroad stock pens. I had just gotten the gate fastened and wired to and started to the depot to order a stockcar to ship these cattle in when up drove Scotty Perth in a one-horse gig. (He referred to this gig as his shay, which he had resorted to as a means of gettin' around since he had lost his leg.)

As Scotty got out of his shay you could tell at a glance that his face was flushed with anger. He raised his heavy voice to a loud pitch, and I am sure that people could hear him all the way to the mercantile. He waved his hands and arms in the air as he threw a pure-blooded Scottish rage. It seemed that the thing that helped to provoke him most to this state of anger was the presence of the old pure-blooded Scotch cow in the herd that he referred to as one of his "lassies."

Scotty was an old man in my eyes, crippled for life, and having some share of trouble. Although I was barely a grown man, he must have seen me as a smart-aleck kid, which made him all the madder.

I had ridden all day without any breakfast or dinner, and it was midafternoon and me and my horse were tired, thirsty, and hungry. I didn't know what to say to Scotty, so I just reined my horse toward the depot and didn't say anything. But as I passed his shay I was stunned when I realized that Scotty Perth was drivin' one of the horses to his shay that I had shod for the doctor. I didn't think he would have the nerve to unfasten the stockyard gates, and if he did he couldn't do anything about that bunch of cattle in his shay, so I rode on about my business.

One of the things that he repeated several times in his broken Scottish brogue was, "I could gather the rest of them in me shay."

The railroad agent, like everybody else, wasn't very friendly and seemed to begrudge the opportunity for the railroad to move another carload of Scotty Perth's cattle. He told me that he would have a car spotted the next mornin' at the stock-pen chute, but he advised me not to load it with the cattle until after noon because the train wouldn't pick up the car until about three o'clock.

I saw Scotty Perth goin' back towards town in his shay as I rode toward the stock pens. The railroad had a stack of alfalfa hay just outside the stock pens for feedin' purposes, so I broke several bales and gave it to the cattle, unsaddled my horse, put him in a separate pen where there was water, and gave him a lot of alfalfa and left my saddle and riggin' laying in the corner of my horse's pen. I covered it with some loose alfalfa I guess out of habit of hidin' it, because I didn't think anybody would bother it.

As I walked to town I felt betrayed over Dr. Turner havin' me shoe Scotty Perth's horse so I didn't go to the drugstore where his office was, and I didn't have any intention of spendin' the night with him. So I went to the country hotel. It wasn't much of a hotel—just an old frame buildin' with eight or ten rooms upstairs and the dining room and lobby and a small pressin' parlor at the back of the buildin' on the ground floor. A cowboy never goes to his room in the daytime.

That cold mornin' ride had caused me to believe I needed a pair of gloves, so I walked over to the mercantile. News had traveled fast and it seemed that ever'body knew there was another load of Scotty Perth's cattle in the stock pens. It was noticeable that the people I saw ignored me or gave me some kind of a distrustin' look.

I asked the clerk in the mercantile for a pair of gloves. He looked in his glove counter and looked at my hands, that are very small, and with a sneer on his face said, "We don't have any gloves for kids."

I put my hands in my pockets and turned and walked out of the store. I started across the street to the hotel, where I intended to eat up half a cow and a bushel of potatoes if they had 'em. I felt that I was that hungry.

Dr. Turner hollered at me when I was about in the middle of the street. I turned and looked at him and walked on across the street. He hollered again to "wait a minute!" adding that he wanted to talk to me.

We stood in the middle of the street, and he said in a rather strained voice, "Why are you stayin' at the hotel? Why don't you come down to the house? You know you are welcome there when you are in town, and I'll have a hard time explainin' to my wife why you would prefer to stay in that old hotel than in her guest bedroom."

I looked him in the eye and cleared my voice and said, "You might tell her that I don't want to shoe any more horses for Scotty Perth."

He said, "Now wait a minute! The horses are full brothers, and Scotty Perth gave my horse to me, and until he lost his leg he had always shod both of 'em. He's so awkward with his peg leg that he can't shoe a horse, and you're the first man that has come along since that could put shoes on them that they didn't interfere with in travelin'. I thought that it might help to ease Scotty's anger if he knew you could shoe a horse."

I said, "So far as I'm concerned, shoein' horses would be a damn poor way of winnin' an argument, and I don't care what Scotty Perth thinks. This stunt has begun to make me wonder whose side you are on."

He looked at me rather painfully as he started to walk back across the street, and in a somewhat bewildered tone of voice he said, "We'll be lookin' for you to come to church Sunday and stay for the party my wife is givin' for the preacher after the services."

I didn't answer him. I turned and walked across to the hotel. I ate up a big batch of grub and went to bed by dark.

The next mornin' I killed time the best I could in a town where nobody spoke to me until the railroad spotted the car at the loadin' chute about eleven o'clock. The cattle had watered good and were full of alfalfa, and I thought they could stand in the car to wait for the train just about as good as they could stand on the ground. There was a ruling by the railroad that all bulls that were shipped in cars of mixed cattle had to be tied with a rope in the car. So I went to the mercantile and bought some big, soft rope to tie these two bulls. I spent part of the mornin' gettin' these bulls in the chute and gettin' the ropes on their horns. They were rank, mean, and bad to fight, but havin' a chute to put them in and then gettin' up on the fence over them was partly play to a cowboy that was used to catchin' 'em outside and havin' to tie them down before he could do anything with 'em. I loaded the cattle about eleven thirty, billed them out, and sealed the car and got on my horse and went back to the mountains.

I didn't do much cowboyin' the rest of that week, and I didn't have any smart ideas about what I was goin' to try next to catch a few of these cattle.

I laid in my bedroll kinda late until the sun came up and it began to get warm. I fed my horses and fixed breakfast, straightened up my camp a little bit, and fooled around until I cooked my dinner. Then I put on my best clothes and saddled old Charlie, my "road" horse, and rode into town just in time for church.

I stood outside under a tree where I tied my horse until the singin' started, then I slipped in and sat down in the back row. Very few people saw me come in, and I don't believe that my presence contaminated the meetin' too much.

At the end of the service, as soon as the preacher said "Amen," I reached down and picked my hat off the floor and started out the door. Dr. Turner's wife was sittin' in the choir where she could see me, and she took a short cut and headed me off before I could get to my horse and gave me a gentle kind of talkin' to and told me in a kind but firm manner to ride on down and put my horse in the barn at her house and stay for the party. I didn't give her much backtalk—just said, "Thank you, ma'm."

It seemed that the whole church came to the doctor's wife's party, and people were visitin' and braggin' on the new preacher. He was a nice kind of young fellow, and I kinda felt sorry for him—just wonderin' if some of those good people might wind up treatin' him like they had me.

Scotty Perth's wife and teen-age daughter were in the

crowd, and you could tell by her talk that she had pure Irish blood. (I learned later Scotty's wife was the daughter of an Irish miner.) Several people asked her about Scotty and why he never came to church any more, and one old man commented on what a beautiful voice Scotty had and how he loved to hear him sing in the choir. I noticed that she was wearin' a beautiful gold watch on a chain around her neck.

I stood around to one side and there were a few of the men who spoke to me in a rather hypocritical tone of voice, I thought. Dr. Turner took time out from his guests to visit with me some, and I tried to be nice (after all, up to a few days ago he was the only friend I had in town besides his wife).

Mrs. Turner opened the door to the dinin' room and the table was loaded with sandwiches, coffee, some kind of sweet punch, and cake. Of course, most of the kids skipped the sandwiches and went on to the cake and punch, and I thought the kids around here are more like people than the grown folks are.

When I went back to the table for seconds, I met Scotty Perth's daughter at the punch bowl. She was a very nice-lookin' young girl and spoke very correct English in a beautiful feminine voice. She glanced at me with a quick eye and said, "You are Ben Green."

I smiled and said yes, and she hastened to tell me that she was Scotty Perth's daughter. As she poured the punch she said, "Father said when you give up or the weather drives you out 'he will gather the rest of the cattle with his shay.'" She said this in a rather arrogant, smart tone of voice; Mrs. Turner heard her and I saw her look at me with an expression of concern.

I set my glass on the table and reached into my vest pocket and handed the young girl a mate to the watch that her mother was wearin' and said, "Give this to your father and tell him that I rode my Texas pony past where his mountain horse fell with a big man and found his watch."

Her voice broke, and she called to her mother, "He has found Daddy's watch."

As her mother looked at it, she said, "Thank heavens! These are the two watches that our daughters gave us on our twenty-fifth wedding anniversary!"

Then the daughter turned back to me, and she suddenly became very embarrassed and her good English broke and she spoke in the mother brogue of her parents and said, "Please do not be too hard on me father. You know he has had much trouble."

I walked through the room and picked up my hat and started for the back door on the way to the barn. Mrs. Turner stopped me at the back door and asked where I was goin'. I told her that I didn't seem to belong at even a church party in Scotty Perth's town and that I would ride out tonight.

She said, "Ben, I am sorry for what's happened," and I said, "It's no fault of yours."

Dr. Turner followed me to the barn and gave me a letter that he said had come to the post office on Saturday, and he had gotten it for me on purpose so that he could give it to me when I came in on Sunday. It was dark, so I thanked him and shoved the letter in my pocket and rode on to the ranch.

He laughingly said as I rode off that half of the people in the church had been out there and looked for that watch while Scotty Perth was in the hospital with his leg, and he wondered how I had managed to find it. That was a secret and I didn't answer him.

The fact was that I was ridin' one day and the sun shone on it and caught my attention. It would be my guess that when Scotty Perth's horse fell from under him, the fall threw it from his pocket and the chain was tangled in a low-hangin' limb just the right height for a cowboy horseback to reach up and untangle it. And while they had looked on the ground for it, it was safely fastened to the limb of a tree.

As I neared the big double gates of the ranch, a thought occurred to me—Why didn't I just take those gates off their hinges to where they wouldn't be swinging back and forth and leave the gates open and take my chances on a few cattle driftin' out into the road? After all, I would rather have 'em in the road than in the pasture—so why leave the gate shut?

These big double gates had a high arched pole at the top runnin' from one gatepost to the other about six feet above the top of the gates. It is true that it was dark, but days and nights seemed to mean about the same to me. So I tied my lariat rope in the middle of each gate one at a time and threw my rope over the big pole that ran from gatepost to gatepost above. Then I tied my lariat rope to my saddle horn and lifted the gate upward off the bolt hinges and then let them drop back to the ground. I pulled the gates back to one side out of the way and propped 'em up against the fence and rode on to camp.

I built up a fire at my camp and read the letter by campfire light. It was from Mr. Merideth at the bank. He was instructin' me to round up all the cattle as soon as possible because of the probability of bad weather, but not to ship any more cattle to the Kansas City market until I wired him and he could wire me back further instructions. I crawled in my bedroll and went to sleep.

When I waked up the next mornin', the weather was still changin' for the worst and as I laid there in my warm bedroll I began to wonder if maybe really the bank was at fault—and if they were, why they had taken advantage of Scotty Perth. With the whole town taking up for Scotty Perth and the fact that I hadn't been able to hire any help from July to late September to ride with me all added up to the conclusion that there was somethin' bad wrong. I had done a good

deal of business with Mr. Merideth and the Kansas City bank, and I couldn't bring myself to think they were at fault. But nobody had tried to fill me in on any of the details of the Scotty Perth deal.

The more I thought about it, the more I realized that it seemed that all the townspeople knew was that Scotty Perth had said the bank was "takin'" his cattle away from him. If there were some undiscovered facts on either side I was the one caught in the middle, and actually all I was tryin' to do was to make more money gatherin' wild cattle than I would ordinarily be paid for common ranch work.

I decided that I had better crawl out of that bedroll and move my camp off of Teepee Rock down into a canyon in the lower pasture. I had already found a good camp place on the west side of the canyon wall. It wasn't exactly a cave—it was just where a big ledge hung over and there was a big curve in the canyon wall that would give protection from the north wind—and bein' on the west side of the canyon the mornin' sun would make it a little more bearable.

I caught the horses that I used mostly for pack horses and spent the day movin' my riggin' and camp to under the ledge in the lower pasture. I took an ax and cut some poles and built a makeshift fence around my camp. My horses were all pets, and I had to protect my feed and my camp by fencin' them out.

When I finished movin' it was late afternoon, but I still had time to drag a few dead trees up by the horn of my saddle for firewood. Dead timber was plentiful and by dark I had enough to last me for a week or two.

The next few days I tried callin' these cattle since it was gettin' cold weather and we had already had some light snow (that hadn't stuck on the ground). I thought it would be gettin' near enough feedin' time of the year if these cattle had ever been fed that they would come to call. Another thing that caused me to think of this—I had remembered that when Scotty Perth throwed his high-pitched voice at the stock pens that old Scotch cow had thrown her head up and bawled a time or two after Scotty had gone.

There was still lots of cattle in the pasture. I didn't know how many, but there was bound to be over two hundred head and I had gathered two hundred and six-teen. For several mornin's I rode down in the valley and tried all the different cow calls that I had ever heard. But I had never gotten a cow to answer nor act like they knew anything about the sound of a human voice.

I waked up one mornin' and a good snow had fallen in the night, but the ground was still a little too warm and unless it got colder this snow would melt by night. I cooked my breakfast and saddled Mustang. I didn't pick Mustang for any particular reason—it was just that he had several days' rest and it was his time to do a good day's work.

My horse was standin' tied close to camp, and I don't know why but I had walked back to stand by the fire and warm while I thought about what to do. A pretty good wind was building up and there was a dark bank formin' in the northeast. It was just a little hard to do a day's ridin' when ever'thing you had tried in the last few days hadn't worked, and I didn't have a new plan to try this mornin'—except I intended to ride down into the valley to see if any cattle had drifted through the gates at the road.

So far as I know I crawled out of a cradle and on to a horse. Although I had a home, I had been a cowboy and drifter and camped all over the Southwest. I had never known any of the pangs of loneliness that I had heard people talk about, and I had never hated anybody and up till now didn't suppose that anybody had been more than a little bit mad at me. But now to have had a whole town and the territory around it to say the least shun me for four months, and for that damn Scotchman to have hated me for every minute that I breathed, was a new and unpleasant experience. With the storm clouds hoverin' over and the wind cold, and so far from Texas, I guess for the first time in my life I must have been lonesome—and it wasn't a good feelin'.

There was a pretty brisk wind blowin' up the canyon and directly I was brought out of this mood by more than a few cattle bawlin' down the canyon below me. This bawlin' increased and got louder, and I could tell that some of these cattle were on the move. Then I heard a faint sound of somebody singin'. I stepped on my horse and went to pushin' down off the canyon wall as fast as was safe horseback.

The singin' began to get clearer and cattle were bawlin'. As I rode out into the openin' where I could see down into the valley there was Scotty Perth on his shay. He had set all the gates open to the corrals and the gate to the trap that joined this pasture and was drivin' his horse at a slow walk to the hooked shay around in the valley and in a high, melodious tone was singin' "Mother MacCrea."

Scotty Perth was a lone wolf and very seldom had anybody to help him with his cattle, and with his beautiful baritone voice he had a call all his own and those half-Hereford Scottish-bred cattle seemed to have a real appreciation for his voice and selection of music. As he rolled the R's and clipped the words and hit the high notes in "Mother MacCrea," all the cattle in that lower pasture were bawlin' and comin' to the valley.

To see all those cattle out in the open was a beautiful sight to me since I had ridden so long and hard, but Scotty Perth's singin' "Mother MacCrea" wasn't necessarily music to my ears.

There was a long strip of slick, shaley rock at the bottom of the slope just before the turf of the valley started, and many a herd of cattle had gotten away because a man can't run a horse across that shaley rock without takin' an awful chance with life and limb, including the possibility of injury to his horse. I circled fast to the east of these cattle, and they were movin' at a good trot and my only hope to offset Scotty Perth's musical ability was to charge these cattle from the east and turn 'em fast through the open gates at the road which was no more than a quarter of a mile west of the gates that he had set to call them through at the north, which would lead them into the valley.

The clouds were movin' in fast and the wind was becomin' variable, which helped me some in that Scotty Perth's singin' wasn't reachin' 'em quite as steadily as it had been when the wind was blowin' up the canyon.

When these cattle were about the same distance from the west gate as they were from Scotty's north gate I had made it around to the east edge of the shaley rock slope. Scotty was drivin' his shay at a slow walk toward the corral gates and had lowered his tone because he knew he had the cattle followin' him. He hadn't yet discovered me because I was ridin' in the timber as best I could behind him until I had gotten to the east side of the shaley rock. The cattle weren't more'n a quarter of a mile from his corrals or from the west gate into the road.

When you are ridin' a horse in a run and he hits a spot of slick rock, it is natural for him to "scotch" in order to steady himself, which increases the possibility of his fall-ing. (If you are ridin' a horse at a trot or fast gait on rock he will extend himself into a run without any thought of "scotching.") This was a slim chance and it might not work, but if it didn't put the cattle in the road it would put them back up in the canyon and it would stop that business I had been hearin' about "gatherin' the cattle in a shay."

I got out on the slick rock with my horse in a trot, took my jacket off, slipped my feet out of the stirrups so in case my horse fell I wouldn't be hung to him, and broke into a top-speed run, swingin' my jacket over my head and squallin' as loud as a Texas cowboy could squall and charged these cattle even before Scotty Perth knew I was in the pasture.

Disturbing weather, variable winds, and fast-movin' clouds add to the nervousness of cattle, and when I ran towards them they were about ready for a stampede anyway. The only glance I got at Scotty Perth durin' the wild ride was when his horse had tried to run away to get out from in front of the chargin' cattle. The herd hit his fence about two hundred yards west of his gates, and as they piled up in a wad some of 'em found the road gate that I had opened the several nights before and the race was on.

I didn't lose a cow gettin' through the gates, but they did knock some of the fence down. I squalled, hollered, and waved my jacket at them until I ran 'em for about five miles. When they had begun to "wind" and slow up, I dropped back to give my horse a breather and let them slow down for the drive to town. Any time you can wind a bunch of wild cattle, it makes 'em easier to handle for the rest of the day.

The cloud had developed into a cold drizzle, and by the time we were halfway to town the roads were gettin' muddy. I had gotten pretty well soaked by now and kind of chilly, and my horse was wringin' wet with sweat and steam boilin' out of his flanks from all the ridin' that I was havin' to do in that heavy, wet dirt.

At the edge of town about two thirty that afternoon, somethin' boogered these cattle, and they made a wild run back up the road toward the ranch. I rode at full speed about three miles in front of 'em, hopin' that nothin' could happen that would cause my horse to fall. The herd finally quit runnin', and after they stopped they milled around in the road awhile and started driftin' back towards town.

In about an hour and a half after the run started, I

had them up close to where they first stampeded and wondered what caused the first run and was hopin' whatever it was would be gone or else that they wouldn't run from it again.

When a bunch of wild cattle go to findin' buggers and runnin', you needn't expect anything but trouble until you get 'em where you started.

I knew Mustang was pretty well spent by now, and I hoped that I wouldn't have to call on him for too much more. I managed to wing the cattle into the railroad right of way and towards the stockyards. I knew that if a train came along or some old woman hung out her washin' or just any damn thing happened, these cattle would run again. But I took my chances and rode just as far away from them on the other side of the railroad as I could. I didn't dare strike a run, so I trotted on to the stock-pen gates and propped them back with some bales of alfalfa hay. The cattle were still comin' and bawlin' as they had been doin' all that day.

The misty rain had turned into a pretty hard rain, which I guess slowed 'em down a little and gave me time to set the stock-pen gates. There wasn't a soul drivin' these cattle from behind, and I was afraid to go around them because I might turn them back. I thought my best chance was to take a few more minutes and break several bales of that alfalfa and scatter it around on the ground in front of the stock pens. I did this, and got on my horse and rode away from the stock pens, and away from the cattle towards the depot and hoped that wet alfalfa would smell enough to stop a bunch of wild cattle that had been on the run all day in the mud and the rain. Sure 'nuff, when the herd began to get into that hay they stopped and went to eatin'. Then I rode way back around them to a pen on the north side of the loadin' chute and pens, crawled over the fence, and went to breakin' alfalfa hay off another stack inside the stock pens.

I knew the hay I broke in front of the stock pens wouldn't last long between what they had eat and what they had tromped into the mud. I broke about twenty-five bales and scattered it, and crawled back over the fence to my horse and then rode back away from them in a walk. I got around them, not to push them, but to wait for them to drift themselves into the stock pens as the hay ran out on the outside. It took a good while, it seemed to me sittin' in that cold rain on a hot horse, waitin' on a bunch of wild Scotch crossbred cows to pen themselves.

When the last cow was in the gates, I rode up as slow as I could and stopped my horse sideways from the gates. I slipped a lariat rope around the first plank of one gate and slipped it through another gate so I could bring them together at the same time. When I started pullin' on the rope and closin' the gates, I did it as quiet as a thief in the dark. When I got the chain around the gates and fastened with the lock, I took the first breath I had had in the last ten minutes.

It was nearly quittin' time for the depot agent, and by reason of the weather nightfall would be soon. I rode up to the depot, and the agent was fixin' to leave and had already locked the door when I stepped off my horse and told him that the stock pens had over two hundred head of cattle in them. That was the first he knew about it. So he unlocked the depot and started to make out an order for stockcars. I told him that I had to wire Kansas City for shippin' instructions, and that we could order the cars in the mornin'.

I sent Mr. Merideth at the bank a night letter saying that I had two hundred and twenty-one head of cattle in the railroad stock pens and none in the Scotty Perth pasture, and would he wire me shippin' instructions.

As I came out of the depot, I noticed the white foamy lather that had almost covered my horse was dryin' and he had begun to quiver.

I rode him in a walk up to the mercantile, which was about a mile and a half away, and bought a wagon sheet and two wool blankets. I took them back to the stock pens with me, and it was almost dark when I decided to change pens with some of the cattle. I put about half of them in a pen on the north side of the loadin' chute and about half of 'em in a pen on the west side of the loadin' chute. Mustang and I got in the crowdin'-pen part of the loadin' chute. This way I was usin' the cattle for a windbreak for me and my horse.

I unsaddled him and covered him up with a wool blanket. Then I tied the wagon sheet to the side of the fence and draped it over him, just leavin' his head stickin' out to where he wouldn't be spooked or boogered by bein' covered up. Mustang was a sensible horse and was rode to exhaustion and had a lot of trust in me. So he let me do all this messin' around him without showin' any sense of uneasiness. It had quit rainin', but the ground was wet underfoot. I carried several bales of alfalfa from the outside pen and broke it up good and shook it out into a pile around under him and got him to move his feet around until I got him upon a pretty good pad of dry hay.

After I had him dried out good, he began to get warm and quit shakin' and shiverin' and began to breathe easy. I found an old bucket and carried him two bucketsful of water, which was all I thought he should have. He groaned and stretched a time or two and laid down on the alfalfa hay with the wagon sheet still stretched over him. But he just laid down like a tired horse ought to sort of settin' down on his haunches and knees with his head and neck out at a restful angle, which is normal for a tired horse. A sick horse stretches out and lays flat on the ground with his body and with his head and legs and will roll and beat his head against the ground.

I felt pretty good about old Mustang and decided I would take that other blanket I bought and roll up in it and lay down to his back. With him on one side of me and a herd of cattle in the pen on the other side of me made a pretty good, warm spot for the night. I waked up a time or two in the night and everything would seem to be all right, and I would doze back off to sleep.

About daylight I began to get cold, and I waked up and saw that Mustang had gotten up and walked out from under the wagon sheet and was standin' up on three legs asleep, which is very normal for a good, healthy horse. The reason I went to all this trouble to dry him off and then to keep him warm was because about a year before this I had gotten into a wild mare drive and rode a good horse in a run most of the day and part of the night. When I unsaddled him, he had walked out in the corral and died before mornin'. I had promised God and all of my good horses that I wouldn't get into that kind of a storm with a bunch of wild stock again. But Scotty Perth and the Scotch-crossed cattle and "Mother MacCrea" had made me forget that until after the ride was over.

I got up and shook myself and looked around. I saw that I still had a bunch of badly drawn cattle in the stock pens and decided I would walk down to the depot to see if I had a wire from Mr. Merideth.

The railroad agent wasn't there yet so I stood around on the south side of the depot, humped up in the weather, and waited for him. It must have been an hour or so until he showed up and unlocked the depot and we went inside.

He got out his telegraph machine and tapped the wire to somebody that he was alive, and they went to givin' him the night's messages. Pretty soon he came through with a night letter from Mr. Merideth.

It started out by instructing me to ship thirty head of the oldest cows to the Kansas City market. The wire further stated that I was to turn one hundred and ninety-one head, or all that I had left after shippin' the thirty, back to Scotty Perth.

Then the last of the wire was addressed to Scotty Perth and stated "when you asked us for additional money last summer, we would have been glad to have made you additional loans provided you would have complied with the new rulings that have been set forth by the federal government whereby all cattle that are submitted to a bank for collateral must be counted, inspected, and appraised. But in your fit of rage you forced the bank to protect its interest by rounding up and selling enough cattle to cover your indebtedness which this final thirty head that we have instructed Ben Green to ship this mornin' will more than finish paying your total indebtedness to this bank. Whatever is left over of that amount will be credited to your account, which so far as this bank is concerned has never been closed. We are instructing Ben Green to turn over to you the hundred and ninety-one head of cattle that are left and are extending to you an invitation to come back and borrow whatever additional money you may need—providing you will leave the rules of banking to the bank and we will leave the matter of ranching to you. Please remember in considering this proposition that you are the one that became angry, and not the bank."

The railroad agent handed me the wire, which was a night letter, and he blew a long sigh of relief and said Scotty Perth ought to be ashamed of himself. I folded the wire and put it in my pocket and immediately gave him an order for an "immigrant car." (An immigrant car is a boxcar [not a livestock car] that is to be loaded with mixed stock, household goods, and anything else that a farmer or stockman would need to move such as implements, etc.) I ordered two barrels of fresh water and twenty bales of hay to be put in the car and told him to spot it at the loadin' dock by the depot for me the next afternoon.

I went by the stock pens and saddled my horse and rode him to town in a slow walk. He was awful sore and stiff and I was goin' to have to be a little careful ridin' to limber him up.

I went to the hotel and was eatin' some breakfast when Dr. Turner came in and sat down on the stool at the counter next to me. News had traveled fast. The railroad agent had beat me to the drugstore and told the story about the Scotty Perth wire.

Dr. Turner broke the silence between us by sayin', "I know about the wire. I wondered what else you had to tell Scotty Perth and the rest of the people of the town."

I had my mouth full of ham and eggs. My horse wasn't hurt too bad from the ride and I was already thinkin' about shippin' out for Texas, so I wasn't in too bad a humor to entertain the doctor's question. I said when I finished my breakfast, "If you've got the time I would like for you to meet me at Scotty Perth's house."

He said, "I wouldn't miss it for the world," and slipped off the stool and went back across the street to his office.

When I came out of the door and started gettin' on my horse I saw Dr. Turner comin' out gettin' in his car. I took my time and rode up in front of Scotty's house and tied my horse to a tree in his front yard and walked up on the porch and knocked on the front door. As Mrs. Perth opened the door Dr. Turner came up on the porch.

Mrs. Perth addressed me by name and then seemed to have lost her speech.

I said, "I want to see *Mister* Perth."

He was listenin' from the livin' room and bellowed, "That kid is not welcome under this roof." Dr. Turner shoved me in front of him and then walked on in front of me and Mrs. Perth and in a firm tone said, "Scotty, shut up and listen to what Ben has to say."

I walked on up to where he was sittin' in a huge chair in front of the fireplace and without speakin' to him pulled the wire out of my pocket and read it to him. He began to break over and hold his head in his hands. Mrs. Perth began to say, "Oh, Scotty, Scotty!" and she repeated it a dozen times or more. The young girl that I had seen at the church party came and sat on the arm of his chair and put her arm around him.

Ever'body was silent it seemed to me for a long time when Dr. Turner said, "Scotty, what do you have to say?"

He got up out of the chair on his peg leg and pronounced Ben like it had an A in it and in his Scottish brogue he said, "Ben, my lad, I have been a mite hard on you."

I was about to explode when I said, "Mite, hell!" I wonder how much a lot would be. There I stood with a wire in my hand giving me just cause and reason to give Scotty Perth the best cussin' that he ever had and would have in Scotland or in America, but my raising at this moment had turned out to be a handicap. I had been taught since a small boy to "behave in the house," "mind your manners and your language in the presence of ladies," and I was already regretting that I had used the word "hell."

I stood there and wished I had Scotty Perth at the stock pens or a wagonyard where I could turn the air blue from there to the horizon, but feeling ill at ease and already embarrassed before Mrs. Perth and Scotty's daughter, I turned and left the room and walked out of the house alone.

I rode slowly back to town and went to the drugstore. It was a long time before Dr. Turner came to town behind me. The druggist had spoken to me that mornin' without calling me mister, so he must have gotten the news too.

Dr. Turner said, "Come back to my office with me." So I followed him back there. He said, "Scotty and Mrs. Perth are pretty bad torn up, and he wonders if there is somethin' he can do to make things better between you and him."

The idea of anything bein' better between me and him sounded repulsive to me, and I told the doctor so.

He said, "Well, there is something else botherin' Scotty. He wanted me to ask you if you would ship some other cattle besides the old pure-blooded Scotch cows and leave them for him to take back to the ranch."

I told the doctor that my instructions were to ship thirty of the oldest cows, and this would probably be my only chance to get some of the mean, mad Scotch blood out of the country and he could damn sure bet that I was goin' to ship every old pure-blooded Scotch cow that there was in the herd.

He said, "Now, Ben, you are bein' mean!" and I said, "What did you expect after four months of lessons in bein' mean?" He didn't answer that.

I went into the mercantile for something, and Mr. Morrow, who owned the mercantile, came over and offered to wait on me. (He had never offered to wait on me before.)

He said, "By the way, I heard you asking for a pair of

gloves a few days ago, and I have found a pair that will just fit you." He was holdin' a pair of beautiful fur-lined gloves in his hands.

I said, "If you heard me the other day why didn't you look for them then." My hands were cracked and sore from holdin' a pair of bridle reins in the weather, but I just stuck them in my pocket and said, "I'm goin' back to Texas where I won't need gloves in the wintertime." As I gave the gloves a quick glance, I said, "Besides, those look like seconds to me."

Back at the stock pens I rounded up my blankets inside of the wagon sheet and stuffed it all under some hay and started to ride out of town. About five or six miles out in the country, Dr. Turner overtook me and had Scotty Perth in the car with him. It was cold but the wind wasn't blowing and I didn't offer to get down off my horse. Scotty got out of the car with his peg leg and came around on the side where I was. He blowed his nose and wiped his chin and looked around. He finally looked up at me and said that he would take it kindly if I would move down to his headquarters and stay a few days and not rush back to Texas. Dr. Turner had rolled the glass down on his car and was listenin'.

He said, "Ben, it's awful cold up there in that camp, and you can't get packed up and out of there in one day, so take Scotty up and stay down at his headquarters."

All the time Scotty was puttin' in how good the beds was, there was plenty of wood, plenty of grub, etc., while the doctor was talkin'.

I said, "It took a wire from the bank to cause him to

notice the weather!" I just reined my horse up and rode off.

I didn't make very good time, and it was way late in the afternoon before I got to camp on old Mustang. But he was limbered up by then and seemed to be gettin' over the wild ride I had put him through the rain and the mud with the wild cattle.

I had all my camp tied up and packed on the horses that were saddled with packsaddles and had halters on my other horses. I tied each halter rope to the tail of the horse in front of him, and I just had a lead rope on the front horse and we came down out of the mountains. We made the trip to town single file.

It was late afternoon when I began to unload my camp and other riggin' into the boxcar that was set at the loadin' dock. It was goin' to be a cold night, and I brought my horses inside and tied five at one end and four at the other end of the boxcar. I kept ole Beauty out to ride until I finally loaded up the next mornin' to leave. I had already watered them so I fed them some oats and gave them plenty of hay to eat and bed down on if they wanted to lay down. I went to the stock pens and got my other blankets and wagon sheet. Scotty's cattle were still there, and somebody had fed them some hay.

The train was supposed to pick up my immigrant car about nine o'clock the next mornin', but I thought I would finish up my chores that afternoon. I knew I was goin' to be in that boxcar with those ten horses for four or five days or maybe a week while we were switched around on different railroad lines until we got back to Fort Worth, Texas.

I rode uptown and laid in a good supply of cheese, crackers, boiled ham, baloney, and the kind of canned grub that you could open and eat without building a fire. I packed all this stuff on Beauty and rode back and put it on the stockcar.

When it was good dark I unsaddled Beauty and put her in with the rest of the horses and was pullin' the stockcar door to when Dr. Turner drove up and said his wife had sent him to bring me to supper.

Ever'body was real friendly and nice, and she was fixin' a big supper. I was playin' with Dr. Turner's younger kids by the fire in the livin' room when in came a bunch of people from around town that had been invited to supper too, including the Scotty Perths.

I kinda bristled up at the sight of him, and I started out of the livin' room to the hall. Dr. Turner dashed out in front of me and here came his wife out of the kitchen, and it looked like they had planned an attack. Dr. Turner said, "Ben, what is the matter?"

I said, "I like most ever'body here, but I was taught not to break bread with people that had misused me or with people that I didn't actually like. In spite of all the good people here I am not fixing to go against my raisin' to get to eat supper with that damn Scotchman." I put on my hat and walked out the door, and walked back to the stock pens and went to bed in good company with my horses.

The next mornin' before the train pulled out, or just about the time the train pulled out, Mrs. Turner, Mrs. Perth, and Dr. Turner came down in the doctor's car and brought a big boxful of food that the women had fixed up for me to eat on my trip back home. I took this and thanked them very much. About that time the train whistle blew, and I waved 'em all good-bye and shut the boxcar door and eat and slept and brushed and curried my horses all the way back to Texas.

BRUSH COWBOYS

BRUSH COWBOYS IN MANY RESPECTS are a different breed from open-country cowboys. They need to think faster, act quicker, be mounted on different kinds of horses, and have a lot more and different rigging than open-country prairie cowboys. Listening to old hands discussing cowboys in the brush country you will hear them talking about different cowhands that they have worked with, and such remarks will crop out as, "He is a good hand with a rope but his skin is thin." This means that if everything is open and favorable, he is a good roper, but his skin being thin indicates that he can't take the abuse of the brush on his body without complaining or flinching to the extent that it interferes with how many cattle he can catch. You will hear other such remarks as, "He's drunk on chimney smoke." This means that he likes to stay at home and enjoys the comforts of a house instead of laying out in camp long enough to wear down and catch outlaw cattle. Then you'll hear some old cowboy speak up and say, "He's a stocker, damn the weather and damn the country. If he ever sees the color of a cow's hide she's caught." This would be a favorable comment on a brush cowhand.

Brush cowboys learn to rope with a very small loop that will just fit over a cow brute's head and horns, and he knows to throw this rope in one swift motion from along the side of his horse since limbs are in his way. The distance across little glades that he will have a chance to rope in are short and there is no time to wind up a loop by throwing it over his head, and there is no distance to waste, and he knows to throw that loop at the *one* first, last, and only chance he is going to have before the steer dives in the brush on the other side of the small glade.

A brush cowboys rigs his horse some different from other cowboys because he is going to hang from the saddle and stand in one stirrup from one side to the other to dodge low-hanging limbs that are too big to stiff-arm out of his way, and there are times that his feet will be in the oddest positions and his cinch rigging front and back must always be tight. However, many brush cowboys do not want breast-harness rigging on a saddle to get in the way.

Winter or summer a brush cowboy will wear a heavy ducking jacket that does not fit tight and most of the time it will be buttoned loose in the front. The old jackets used to have reinforced sleeves from the wrist to the elbow. These heavy ducking jackets are not worn for warmth;

they are worn for protection against limbs of all kinds but especially against mesquite, catclaw, and other growth that are abundantly supplied with thorns or stickers.

Leather chaps or leggings were the common rigging for a man horseback even though he had heavy ducking britches on. The legs actually need more protection in a thicket than the body because a rider can swing his body many different ways to dodge but his legs are pressed against a horse and have very little leeway to get away from thorns and such, which is the reason you see leather on a man's legs in the brush. Various attempts have been made by cowboys to drape and fasten loose-hanging leather over the shoulders and forelegs of a horse but none have been very satisfactory. I have seen and have ridden many a horse out of the thicket after a hard day's work with much of the hair gone from the forelegs and shoulders and sometimes a little blood oozing from the many scratches.

I have known and seen brush cowboys work that had lived in the big thickets so long and were stove up so bad that some of them have to lead their horse to a ditch or a stump or a rock in order to reach their stirrup to get in their saddle, but they get limber and more alert with every limb they dodge. Song and stories have been written about cowboys but little tribute has ever been paid to the toughness of a man that has lived horseback in the big thorny brush thickets of the Far Southwest.

Brush horses have greater instinct about smelling and trailing wild cattle than open-country horses have. I have ridden horses that were bred and born and native to the brush countries that could take a man to a cow the man could neither see nor hear but the horse could smell. I have ridden around a big thicket and been ready to give up that there was anything in the thicket when my horse would refuse to rein away and leave because he could smell a cow or calf that had a wound and a case of screwworms and was lying down and well concealed in that thicket. When an old brush horse refuses to rein away from a dense thicket, you had better listen to him because he can smell better what is in that thicket than you can see; and cattle can hide and be so motionless that they can make no noise that can be picked up by the human ear.

Big horses are not desirable in the brush country because they put the rider up tight against the limbs and the heat of the brush and they also experience more difficulty getting their own bodies through and between closely growing trees.

Brush cowboys use many different kinds of rope in trapping wild cattle and bringing them to a corral or out into the open. The first ropes used by brush cowboys were platted from rawhide or from horsehair. Rawhide ropes are never as stout or as tough as we usually would think of anything that is made out of rawhide because it has to be split and spliced together so often that there are "thick" places in the rope and the thin parts of a hide will naturally plat into a weak spot in the rope. The very best rawhide ropes have to be used carefully and be left loose at one end where you can give slack to keep them from breaking rather than to be tied hard to the saddle horn or to a tree or whatever you are tying to. Horsehair ropes of the same size are a lot stouter than rawhide. Horsehair plats smoother and makes a prettier rope; however, it is hard on the human hand when you are trying to use it and does not have the right weight to have a good feel and throw to it.

The early-day standard of perfection for all ropes has been and still is the Silk Manila rope, and the first one that I ever saw was made by the Plymouth Rope and Cordage Company and was known as Plymouth Silk Manila. These ropes came in three or four strands. The three-strand rope was the most used and the best handling size. Silk Manila is an extremely hard rope and very stiff when it is new and cowboys have resorted to a number of different ways of breaking in a Manila lariat rope. Tying one end to a tree and pulling the other end with a saddle horn; or tying one end to a tree and the other end to a tree and wetting the rope and letting it dry stretched was another means of breaking in the Silk Manila. Probably the most common method was to tie one end of the rope to a saddle horn when you were riding down the road or going across pasture and not driving any livestock, and the constant bouncing and jerking over the ground would limber up a rope. After a cowboy gets a Silk Manila properly broke in where it has the right feel and is limber enough to throw but stiff enough for the rope to stand open until it catches on a cow, he gets very particular about what else he does with that rope. He doesn't let it get wet unless he has to and is careful about tying knots anywhere up and down the rope that might cause it to form a kink that would make it throw or do up bad. Certain ropes become favorites in the hands of a cowboy just like certain tools or instruments become favorites in the hands of mechanics or engineers.

Many new materials have been made into ropes in recent years. Linens have been woven into stock ropes and dipped into various wax and oil preparations in order to give them weight and keep them from absorbing moisture. Cotton ropes have been tested with various treatments but have never been satisfactory as a throwing rope to catch livestock. There have been other materials that attempts have been made to use for ropes, and the latest near-success in a new rope material is Nylon. The strength of Nylon rope is without question, but the feel, handle, and the throwability of Nylon will never compare to the good touch of a well-broke-in Silk Manila rope.

When a brush cowboy sets a snare over a trail, he takes lots of time and wraps wild vines around the rope for disguise and hangs the rope over the trail in such a manner that it is held open by limbs. This needs to be a big soft rope that would not be easily pitched over to one side, so when it is touched it will fall loosely around a steer's head, whereas with a hard Manila rope the loop would stand open and a cow brute would throw it or cause the loop to pitch over to one side like a hoop would. Brush cowboys use big heavy ropes that are also soft, and when I say big I mean an inch or more in diameter. This rope is used, after a cow has been snared or roped in the brush, to tie around her neck and tie to a lead oxen around his neck and shoulders or sometimes to a burro. This lead oxen or burro has been trained to take an out-law cow brute to the headquarters or to a certain set of holding pens maybe several miles from where the cow brute has been caught. This big soft rope won't hurt the outlaw cow and won't hurt the lead oxen that is dragging the outlaw cow. It will be big enough that any unusual wear or pull on a tree or across rocks could not break or wear into it easily. It will take patience on the part of the lead oxen and patience on the part of the brush cowboy, but in a course of time, maybe two or three days, the lead oxen will finally show up at the place where he has been fed good feed and clean water and properly cared for, and he will be dragging some part of what's left of that wild cow brute.

Maguey ropes made from long dry fibers out of cactus plants are small ropes that were referred to by cowboys as being "hot" because if one slips through your hand the rope burn is more severe than from any other kind of rope. These little maguey ropes are hand-made individually in Mexico and vary in length from forty to as much as sixty feet and are platted from a starting point and will have no knot in it. The finishing end will be finished into a hondo for the unfinished end to be passed through the small loop which gives you a swinging loop to be used. These ropes have a good feel and throw with a remarkable degree of accuracy. Because of the fact that they are usually platted small in diameter, a brush cowboy seldom ever ties one hard and fast in a double half hitch to his saddle horn. Instead, when he ropes, he dallies as much as two rounds on his saddle horn and leaves a lot of rope behind the dally that he can feed out when a cow hits the end of the rope in order to reduce the sudden snap that will break a maguey rope. This is one of the reasons that they are made so much longer than Silk Manila ropes.

Pages more could be written about the various processing of ropes made from different kinds of material and lengthy discussions could be gone into about the rawhide and horsehair ropes of Mexico and the Southwest to the camel-hide ropes of the desert, but the long, hard, flexible fibers of the grass families still make the most desirable ropes for all purposes and can be woven hard or soft and then platted to as many strands as is necessary for strength.

THE MARION
PASTURE

I HAD GATHERED A BUNCH OF OUTLAW
steers out of the Kiamichi Mountains for Old Man Buck
Hurd of Fort Worth, Texas. I wired him the day before
that I was loading out for Forth Worth.

I loaded my saddle horses in one end of a car by building a partition between my horses and the steers. The train pulled into the Fort Worth stockyards about four thirty in the morning. I was riding in the caboose, so I waked up and helped unload the cattle and my horses. I took my five saddle horses across Exchange Avenue from the cattle stockyards to the horse and mule barns where I could feed and water and leave them in a good pen. When I had finished taking care of my horses, I went back to the Livestock Exchange Building to wait for Old Man Hurd to come to his office. In those days the Fort Worth stockyards were a great central market for the entire Southwest, and the blackboard in the lobby that morning showed 22,000 cattle, 7,000 calves, and other numbers for sheep and hogs that I do not remember. This was the day's run and by daylight all the stockyards' helpers and all the livestock commission men were busy. Then later in the morning the office help would show up around eight o'clock.

Old Man Buck Hurd had graduated to the status of office, but he showed up about seven o'clock. Buck Hurd was a product of the old West. Hardships had been the pattern of his way of life for the first fifty or sixty years, and now he wore the best of store-bought clothes, but even that could not hide the fact that he was a tall, skinny, rough, old, bowlegged, buck-kneed cowboy who had spent more of his life in the saddle than he had out of it and more of his nights sleeping on the ground than in a bed. His eyes were small, black, and beady and set so far back under his forehead that he could have rode in the brush without having to bat his eyes, as a limb could never have reached them. His face was bony and his nose had been broken when a horse fell with him, and had grown back about the shape of a quarter circle brand, which made him look like he had just smelled something that he was turning the end of his nose away from. He seldom smiled, but when he did the corners of his mouth turned down instead of up. He had been mad most of his life about something or at somebody and until recent years was bad to fight. However, he had said that he had learned to argue more and fight less as he grew older. He was known to be fair in his dealings and his judgment in the steer business was well respected by cattlemen all over the Southwest. He looked up at me as though he were surprised that I had gotten back alive. But instead of saying something nice about being glad to see me or any of that sort of pleasant conversation, his raspy ole voice blared out, "Where's my steers?"

We walked out through the Exchange Building into the stockyards and looked at the cattle that I had shipped in from Oklahoma. There was forty head of big, rough, aged, plain-quality steers that had gone wild and gotten away in the spring when all the other cattle were shipped out to the Flint Hills country of Kansas to be fattened for fall market. I had taken the job of gathering these wild cattle for $5 per head, which was at that time an extremely high price, and you might well know when an old cowman would pay such a price that the cattle had almost been a lost cause and he had given up being able to gather them by reasonable means. Of course, he counted the steers at a glance and said there ought to be forty-three. I told him that I had found the carcasses of two other steers that had died, but that I didn't believe the third steer had ever been in the Kiamichi Mountains. We went back to the office of the Evans-Snyder-Buell Commission Company where Old Man Buck headquartered. We were sitting in the outer office at a table, and he was writing me out a check and finally confessing that he hadn't believed that I would gather even as many as forty head.

About that time a Mr. Girard from Kansas came into the office, and Buck said, "Here's another job for you," as he called Mr. Girard by name and motioned for him to come over to the table. He introduced me to Mr. Girard and explained to him that I was the boy that would gather his wild cattle. In the conversation it developed that Mr. Girard had leased a pasture for several years in far southwestern Texas where he wintered big, aged steers in the mild climate of the Southwest with little expense; then shipped them in the spring to the bluestem grass country of northern Oklahoma and Kansas to be fattened. This was a common livestock operation in those days and was carried on extensively by cattlemen that were commonly referred to as "steer cattlemen."

Mr. Girard was giving up the pasture that he had leased for several years. During that time each year he had failed to gather the wildest of the cattle out of each bunch until he had an accumulation of wild cattle as the only ones remaining.

This was late September, and he said that his lease ran out the first of November and that he would not be as much interested in paying to have these cattle gathered as he would be in selling them real cheap, range delivery. Buying wild steers in rough country, range delivery, was risky business, and it was seldom that you could find a cowboy wild enough or foolish enough to make such a trade. We talked on about these cattle and Old Buck Hurd told me how big the oldest ones would be and some of them could weigh 1,500 pounds. It was anybody's guess as to how many steers were actually in this big pasture, but Mr. Girard said that he was short more than seventy steers from what he had turned in the pasture over a period of four years and what he had gathered out. Assuming that some of them may have died, he believed that there would be at least fifty steers and could be more.

He offered to take $1,000 for fifty head or more, range delivery. This didn't sound too interesting to me, so Old Man Buck made a big speech saying he would grab the proposition if he was my age. I always got along with Old Man Buck probably because I talked back to him. I told him that if it was going to make me look like him at his age that I didn't want the cattle. Of course, I laughed when I said it, and he grinned barely enough to let me know that the remark didn't make him mad. I told Girard and Old Buck that I didn't have $1,000 to buy the cattle with, and Old Buck blared out that I had $200 because he had just given me the check. Well, he didn't know it but that was the only $200 I had, and I had worked a month gathering his cattle with five head of horses for that money. He told Mr. Girard that I would be in town all day (he didn't know whether I would be or not) and that he thought he would make me take the steers and I could get the $1,000 to pay for them if I wanted to buy them. Well, that was news to me, and after Mr. Girard left the office I asked Old Buck, "Where do you think I would get $1,000?"

He said, "Well, Ben, you don't need but $800 and that bunch of steers could make a lot of money and you just as well be gathering that bunch of cattle for yourself as some other bunch that you'd just be getting paid for by the head. So we're going down to the North Fort Worth Bank and I'm going to sign your note for the money."

This little gesture was further proof that he was neither as tough as he looked nor as mean as he sounded, and even though he would never say so, he must have appreciated me getting his wild cattle or he would not have been trying to make this trade for me.

We walked down to the North Fort Worth Bank, which was in the next block on Exchange Avenue. He introduced me to a bald-headed, good-natured banker and explained to him that I needed $800 and told him why and what I was going to do with the money. I put in my argument that I needed $900 because I needed $100 to use as expense money. Old Buck had been an old starved-out cowboy and said that $25 was enough expense money. So he and I had a big argument, well punctuated with profanity and expressions that were peculiar to the cattle business. The banker went to writing out a note for $900. Old Man Buck glanced over with his Indian-like eyes, and just in defiance of losing the argument said, "Damned if I'll sign it!"

The banker smiled and said, "Buck, you don't have to sign it; Ben's going to get a bill of sale when he pays for the steers and I'm going to attach it to this note, and you've lost the argument because the boy will need $100 to feed his horses and himself while he catches that bunch of wild cattle."

We walked back up to the stockyards and Old Man Buck pretended that he had something else to do and I thanked him for the check and introducing me to the banker and walked out on the livestock exchange to watch the usual course of business, see how cattle were selling, what classes were in most demand, and maybe run on to an old friend or two to pass the time of day with. After all, I had been camped in the brush several weeks and needed to do a little jaw work with some more cowboys.

The North Fort Worth Stockyards were built with the railroad tracks running through the lower third of the yards, cutting it off from the north part, which was the main part of the stockyards. There was a high footbridge built over the railroad tracks from the south side to the north side of the yards, and anytime you were lookin' for somebody on the stockyards, you made it to the high bridge; from there you could see the entire yards and spot whoever you were lookin' for. It was a little like climbin' a windmill to look over the pasture. The stock pens had walkways built around over the top of 'em and the business and visiting of the day took place on these walks.

I was standin' on the high bridge lookin' over the yards and DeWitt Kerr came along. I had cowboyed for

DeWitt and he and I always had some pleasant conversation for each other. This morning I was glad to see him 'cause I wasn't too certain about this big steer deal that Old Man Buck was 'aggin' me into.

I told DeWitt about gatherin' the steers for Old Man Buck in Oklahoma and about the proposition that I had been bannered with that morning. DeWitt was always my friend, and he knew I needed to make the money and he told me he thought it would be all right if I could get enough time on the contract to gather the steers. He cautioned me that that might be rougher country than I had been used to workin'. I told him about the visit down to the bank and he said that if he were me, when he started to pay the man he would just take him down and let the banker pay him and get the bill of sale drawn up to suit the banker. Well, this was a good lesson in business, one that I hadn't thought of, so I thanked him as he ambled down the other side of the stairs, off the bridge; he waved at me as he left and wished me good luck.

About noon I was standing around in the livestock exchange lobby when Mr. Girard walked up; I guess he knew I was lookin' for him. He walked right straight over to me and asked me if I was ready to buy the steers and emphasized the phrase "range delivery." I explained to him that I thought it would be best if the banker closed the trade, so "let's go down to the bank." He and the banker had a short visit. The banker drew up a good bill of sale for all the cattle in the Marion pasture that were wearing the brands that Mr. Girard had turned in the pasture through the years that he had leased it. This was a great long list of brands, since he was a trader and had bought all the steers that he turned in from all over the cow country.

I got on the Red Ball bus that afternoon and went to Weatherford and spent the night with my folks and told them that I was headed for South Texas to gather another bunch of steers.

I went back to the stockyards the next day, and was eatin' dinner in the old Stockyards Hotel. As I started to leave, a man spoke to me that was wearin' a railroader's outfit. They didn't dress like cowboys or other workin' people; they had their own kind of riggin' and it was easy to tell a railroad man without askin' him where he worked. This fellow had been an old schoolmate of mine. We visited a few minutes, and I told him that I was about to start out of town with my saddle horses to go to South Texas to gather wild steers that I had bought "range delivery." He said that his crew was fixin' to pull a bunch of livestock cars out of the stockyards that were being fresh-bedded to be deadheaded to Brownwood, Texas, and that if I jumped my horses into one of those empty cars, he didn't believe that he would find them before we got to Brownwood.

I said, "I don't know whether my horses will jump or not, but you might look for me when you go to cut loose in the stockyards in Brownwood."

'Course I got the hint real fast that he wouldn't mind haulin' my saddle horses one hundred fifty miles. It would save me about six days' ride. I shuffled across to the horse and mule barns. My horses were rested and full and ready to do something, so I threw my saddle on one horse and my pack rig on another horse, and led the other three across North Exchange Avenue into the railroad part of the stockyards. Sure enough, my horses jumped in one of those empty cars without half tryin'. I shoved the stock-car door almost to, and set around on a fence and waited to see the train come in. It wasn't but a few minutes until it bumped the cars and hooked on. I hopped up in with my horses, and by the middle of the afternoon we un-loaded in Brownwood. That was about the fastest six-day ride I ever made by horseback!

It took me another week to drift down into the far southwestern part of the hill country to the Marion pas-ture. This pasture had about 9,000 acres in it laying east and west the long way. The east end of the pasture joined the river. More than 7,000 acres of this trace was in two long, deep, rough canyons that joined at the river and ran back up into the pasture toward the prairie. About 300 acres on the west end of the tract was cut off from the main body of the land by a country road. It was up on a high prairie and had a windmill and an old shed-type barn about twenty feet long and twelve feet deep facing south that was built out of rock with a tin roof on it. There were some small corrals there around the windmill, and this shed was where I made my camp.

This old rock shed hadn't been used in a long time, and I could tell at a glance that there was several wasp nests and maybe some other kind of varmints in those old rock walls. The rock walls had been laid in wall fashion and were about two feet thick, but they weren't put together with any cement. I had had experience in campin' in old barns, and knew that I might have some company there, so first thing I did was to gather some loose dry lumber and take my ax and cut some green live-oak limbs and small bushes and build up a smoke fire on the south side, which was the front of this old shed. There was a little breeze blowin' and I fanned the smoke back up in under the shed. I drove out a wad of wasps and bees about as big as a full toe sack. I went around on the back side and killed two rattlesnakes as they crawled out of this rock wall; I saw a coon leaving off at the east side. With this little job of house-cleanin' finished, I made my camp in under the shed, scraped the coals up from this first fire, fed and watered my horses and cooked some supper, and went to bed a little after dark. I needed to get some rest and get myself located 'cause tomorrow I intended to see that $1,000 worth of cattle that I owed for.

Next mornin' I saddled a horse and decided to ride the outside fences of the big pasture and get the lay of the land before I begun to outsmart this bunch of outlaw cattle. DeWitt was right when he told me it was rougher country than I was used to workin'. The canyons had a rimrock around the top of 'em where they broke off from the prairie, and then a deep sloping wall that disappeared under a dense growth of live oak, mesquite, and cedar. As I rode down the canyon wall on the south side and started around the east side, I ran into an awful lot of dead timber, some standin' and some that had fallen. This was goin' to add to the roughness of the rock and canyons that I was going to have to ride over to catch wild cattle.

I saw the brush shake in front of me a few times during the mornin' and just caught a glimpse of some great big cattle. They were sure wild and stayed out of sight in the dense underbrush of those great big canyons. This was going to be a rough job 'cause these cattle didn't have to leave the canyons to come to water. Water was plentiful up and down the river and there were springs up and down the canyons, so there was going to be no central point that I could wait for and trap or rope these cattle. It seemed that they had been run and hunted a lot and were allergic to the sight of a man on horseback.

I topped out on the northwest corner of the prairie and rode back to my camp to fix dinner and try to get some bright idea about how to catch these wild cattle.

That afternoon I went down in the pasture and made lariat-rope snares over the most common traveled trails. I took time to wrap grapevines and other leaves around the lariat ropes and hang the loop open over the trails with limbs and string, then run the main rope back to the trunk of a tree and took a big double half hitch on the trunk of a tree. That would be a knot that I could undo and it would be one that the steers couldn't get away with the rope on. I made seven of these snares before sundown and went back to camp. Of course the cowboy is subject to wishful thinking, and I just thought that I could nearly catch enough cattle out of this pasture in a few days, with snares, to pay back the money and the rest of them would be profit.

I rode out on the edge of the rimrock by sunup the next morning and studied the brush in the canyon below. I did see the color of hair mingled among the trees on some different bunches of cattle, but by the time I could ride to them they would have heard me and would be long gone. I saw some bushes moving where one of my snares were, so I kicked my horse off the edge of the rimrock and started to that particular spot. I heard some bawlin' and carryin' on before I got to my snare and I could just imagine that I had a big one. I rode up a little cautiously to find a fat suckin' calf that weighed about 350 pounds. This discovery messed up my plans. I had a bill of sale on steer cattle; nobody up to now had mentioned any cows or any calves or anything else in that pasture besides steers.

It was plain to see at a glance that this calf had never been branded, and I had caught him in my snare and it had bawled and bellered and spread the alarm and put the wild cattle on notice that there was something up.

There was a cow standing back down the canyon about two hundred yards with her head stuck out of the thicket. She hadn't called to the calf, but she was watchin'. I stepped down off my horse to untie the calf from the tree and try to lead it down out of the thicket. After all, I didn't see much point in turnin' it loose; it belonged to somebody and it didn't belong to my steers. I thought it would be smart to at least take it up and put it in that little pasture across the road.

This little pasture across the road had a high net-wire fence around it and was going to be a place to hold whatever I caught to put in it. About the time I stepped off my horse, this old cow came out of the brush and bawled and started after me. I got the rope untied and dallied around my saddle horn just as she horned my horse in the side.

This old horse was named Mustang. He was a well-bred horse and had no mustang blood in him, I am reasonably sure. I had caught him as a two-year-old in northern Arizona out of a bunch of mustang horses, which accounts for his name. He was a blood bay, 15 hands 2 inches tall, and would weigh about 1,150 in hard-usin' condition. He was one of the most willing horses that I ever owned, and he knew that calf was tied to him and he had determined not to get in a storm by flinchin' from that old cow. She raked him across the side with her horns and knocked a little hair and cut a little hide, but didn't really do him any serious damage. The calf began to bawl and run when we pulled 'im and drove 'im and jerked 'im over little brush, medium-size rocks, and drug 'im around a few big ones. By the middle of the morning I pulled him across the road and took the rope off of 'im in the little pasture. The old brindle nondescript common kind of a cow didn't follow us out of the timber. When she hit the opening she turned back.

I rode the rest of the day. I could see a few cattle in front of me, but I never could get them in the proper angle to force them out of that canyon. I had thought if I could push some against the fence that maybe I could booger them into comin' out to the top of the prairie. About all I got out of that day's ride was somebody else's calf and more than a common amount of discouragement from these brush-wise steers.

In about two days this old cow began to bawl and came to the fence and begin to try to get across the road to her calf. When I rode out to pull her through the gate, she would go back to the canyon. I wasn't hankerin' to put a rope on this old cow because she had long, sharp horns; the calf hadn't sucked in two days and her bag was pretty sore and she was beginning to get real mad. I just got to thinking that I was tryin' to get cattle out of that pasture and keepin' that fence up by the road wasn't too smart, so I put in about half a day takin' the fence down along the road from the north corner about a quarter of a mile and from the south corner about a quarter of a mile. After all, if I ever did drive some cattle up that fence line, I ought to make it handy for 'em to get out of the pasture. But I didn't take down the fence that was parallel to the gate to the little pasture. If I ever got anything in that lane I wanted the gate on the other side of the little pasture to be the only thing open.

That night the old cow came up, found her way out in the road, and was smellin' her calf through the fence the next morning. It was easy to open the gate to the little pasture, ride into the big pasture, and go around her and ease her up to where she would go in with her calf. That was the fourth day, and I had caught one cow and calf that didn't belong to me and wouldn't pay on that $900 I owed.

I rode after and aggravated these cattle for several days, and I had begun to get some in about three bunches, but the harder I rode the smarter they got and the farther they got away from me. I kept 'em so busy in the daytime that they had to graze at night. We had some moonlit nights and a few of these cattle came up on the prairie where the grass was better than it was in the canyon. I had sneaked around behind 'em when the wind was right and they couldn't smell me, and I had managed to rope three steers in the moonlight in three nights. It was almost an all-night job to rope one steer and get 'im across the road in the little pasture before the moon went down and the night got dark again. Two of these steers that I had caught would weigh over 1,200 pounds apiece and were great big ole yellow Mexican-looking longhorn kind of cattle that would bring about $50 apiece on the Fort Worth market. This, in cowboy arithmetic, meant that there might be $2,500 worth of cattle in that horse-killin' canyon if I could just figure out some way to bring 'em out on top of the prairie.

There was an old man that had a little farm and a small pasture that joined this place at the river on the northeast corner of the fence line. I rode down one day and got acquainted with 'im. His name was Eness Jarrera. He had been a great old cowboy that time and hard work had overtaken. All he did now was to raise a few sheep and goats and he had three or four cows and raised a little crop of feed stuff for his stock and for himself.

He knew right off that I was the rider that had been in the big pasture tryin' to catch the steers. He was very friendly and interested in how I was getting along. I told him about the cow and calf. He brightened up considerably and told me there were two more cows with calves; that these had gotten away from him when they were heifers, and, since he was too old to fight the brush and ride horseback, that he had just had to let them go and didn't know that he would ever get them back. Well, I told him I had one cow and calf caught for him and he was welcome to 'em. He was pleased about this, but he said they were too wild to bring back to his small pasture, that they wouldn't stay, and that if I would keep 'em and ship 'em with my cattle, that he would rather have what money they would bring than to have the cattle back. Well, this was all right with me, and I was glad that I had at least caught some of his cattle. I knew that he probably would be glad to have the money that the cattle were worth.

He told me much about Mrs. Marion, who owned this pasture, and that he had worked for her husband when they operated the old ranch. He said that she lived in Austin and was a grand lady, and that sometimes he got a letter from her and that she always sent him something for Christmas. I had already begun to worry about my time runnin' out at gatherin' these steers, and I asked him if he thought she might lease me the pasture for a few more months if I needed it. He didn't venture an opinion, but he did say that she was a fine and reasonable woman. This was some consolation, but it didn't exactly fit my plans to camp there under that rock shed all winter to catch these cattle.

About two weeks later I took stock of my situation. I had five good horses and four of them were crippled. It took about half of my time every morning and later every afternoon to doctor my crippled horses, and the one horse that was able to carry me was a light-boned, small, good traveling horse but not big enough to rope big steers. I had drug a steer on ole Beauty, my standby, one night that was so big and rough and heavy that it had bruised her withers where the saddle sat, and she was so swelled and sore that I was afraid to ride her, thinking I might make it worse. I had caught a steer on Mustang just as it leaped off of the rimrock and started down the canyon wall. Mustang set all four feet and kept his balance and let that steer drag him halfway down the canyon and never flinched. When he finally got on level ground he stopped the steer and we drug 'im back out. I had roped him around the horns and he didn't choke, which left him with an awful lot of fight in 'im. I began to notice a little blood on the rocks and I saw the steer wasn't hurt, and I knew Mustang must be skinned somewhere. After about a three-hour battle I got the steer in the small pasture and got my rope off of 'im, and I stood and looked at Mustang. When he slid down the canyon wall the rocks had torn the hide off of the back of his hind legs from his ankles to his hocks. He could have bounced forward and saved his legs and maybe got jerked down, or maybe let the steer get away, or have gotten us both hurt, but his nerve and his "know-how" had gotten us out of the storm with the steer, but he was goin' to be laid up with sore legs for a good while.

I ripped the sleeves out of a duckin' jacket and cut 'em open a little wider at the cuff and slipped 'em over his back legs up above his hocks and tied 'em with a string. I kept some salve rubbed on 'em, and these jumper sleeves kept the flies and the dirt and the trash off of 'em. I dressed them twice a day. I washed the sleeves at night when the insects weren't workin' and put them back on in the morning before fly time.

Another good horse named Charlie had dived into a deep thicket tryin' to help me rope a steer when a snag of a dead tree laid his brisket open. My fourth horse had clawed a shoe off in the rocks and took part of the foot wall with it. I had to cut an old hat up and lace it around his foot in order for him to stand the pressure of moving around a little bit, to eat and drink, on that foot.

When a wild cowboy in a rough country after wild cattle gets most of his horses crippled, he's about out of business. That note I signed was drawin' interest and the lease on the pasture was runnin' out. I laid around camp and doctored my horses and rested and looked at the nine head of cattle that I had caught out of the sixty, seventy that were in that pasture; it seemed to me like that I was losin' so fast that time was goin' to keep me from breakin' even.

Early one morning I boiled some water on the fire, shaved with a pocketknife, and went down in my bedroll and brought out my Sunday-best pair of britches and my last clean shirt. I got dressed up as best I could and rode into town, left my horse in a little pasture behind the feed store, and caught the Red Ball stage to Austin. I had decided that I needed to have a talk with Mrs. Marion.

About middle of the mornin' I walked into the Driskill Hotel. I stood around a little bit. I sort of got up my nerve and walked up to the desk and asked if Mrs. Marion lived there. The old gentleman at the desk said, "Yes, her suite is 312." I said, "Thank you."

I walked back out in the center of the lobby and stood

around until I found the stairway. Now I have seen a few stairways in cow-country hotels, and the most of 'em run up the side of the wall about the same angle as a loadin' chute and not much wider, and it didn't seem that that hotel had one. As I stumbled around and looked around, though, I found a stairway that I wasn't quite used to. It was about as wide as a country road and was curved up the side of the wall sort of like a trail going around a mountain, and it was covered with a rug that looked like dead curly mesquite grass when it beds down on the ground for the winter. People may not stop to think about it, but a cowboy always dreads a stairway. If he's actually spent his days in the saddle and his nights on the ground, his legs are awful stiff, his ankles just bend front and back and his knees just bend sideways and his hips are about solid.

I eased over to the rail side of the stairs and started pullin' with one hand and lettin' my legs follow. I found number 312—I took my hat off and had the brim rolled up in a tight grip when I knocked on the door. A kind of plain-lookin' youngish lady came to the door. I asked for Mrs. Marion. She didn't say anything to me but turned and said, "There's some boy wants to see you."

Mrs. Marion said, "Well, show him in."

You could tell by the tone of her voice she was a little impatient with this woman that answered the door. When I walked in you could tell at a glance that Mrs. Marion was all that old Eness had said she was and more too. She stuck out her hand and introduced herself, and I told her who I was. She made a motion to one of those flimsy kind of chairs that I wasn't too sure it would do to sit on, but anyway I took my chances. She didn't offer to "take my hat." That is an awful mistake that nice people make when they are tryin' to make a cowboy feel at home. He hates to give up his hat. He might want to leave in a hurry, or fight a fly, or hit a man, or scare a horse, and he never likes to turn loose of his hat. But in a few minutes she had me so much at ease that I had throwed that hat on the floor beside my chair. In our conversation I had gotten the news over to her about the trade on the steers and about the bad luck I was havin', and I told her about my horses bein' crippled, which was the reason I had come to see her to get more time on the pasture. She was a very attentive listener, and you could tell she was an old ranchwoman and was sympathetic with my plight.

She had asked me where I was from, and I told her Weatherford, Texas. Then she asked me did I know Barto Hood. Barto Hood was the town's gruffest character and most prominent lawyer, and was a friend of mine on the occasions that he chose to get after me about something that I was doin' or that he thought I should do. I was sorry to learn that she knew him. I told her that I knew him, but that I wasn't braggin' about it, and she thought this was rather funny. She said that she had gone to college with him at the old Veal Station College and from what I said, he must still be his normal self. Once in a while I guess I said something funny, and when she threw her head back and laughed, you could tell it did her good. It didn't sound like a man but she didn't try to snuff it out like a woman sometimes does, either. It was hard to guess whether she was middle-aged or an old woman. She gave off lots of sunshine, and if there had been any frost or shadows in her life, she kept 'em brushed away.

The girl, Eloise, was a niece of hers and hadn't entered into the conversation but had just sat there and listened. It was gettin' about dinnertime by now and Mrs. Marion suggested that Eloise take me down to the dining room for dinner. I went to alibi-in' a little bit, and this old ranchwoman said, "Well, if you came by my ranch you'd stay for dinner and you've got to eat somewhere, so you two go on down to the dining room and come back when you're finished."

This didn't suit me too much, but I didn't know of anything I could do about it, so we went down to the dining room.

This Eloise was pretty dull company. I have seen horses like her, no speed and no sparkle, that go through life walking with their heads down. If they ever look off or strike a trot they stumble or do something wrong. If the grub hadn't of been better than her conversation, I couldn't have stood neither one of 'em.

Well, I finished up this little batch of town chuck, and we went back upstairs. Mrs. Marion carried on a little light conversation for a few minutes, and I glanced at her and saw that she was lookin' me over. My best Sunday britches that I had on, of course, were saddle-marked inside, my boot heels were spur-marked, and both my hands were rope-burned. I had spent the summer outside and my hair and my face was pretty well burned up by the sun, and I am sure that to that gracious lady I must have been a pitiful picture.

She broke the silence by sayin' that she had called Barto Hood on the phone.

I said, "Well, I guess I just as well get my hat and go if you're gonna abide by what Barto said, because if he ever knew anything good to say about me, he's still got it—he never said it to me."

She thought that was funny, and told me that Barto had been very complimentary and had assured her that if the cattle could be caught that I would catch them, and to give me time. She explained to me that it was hard to lease a ranch with the reputation that had built up around the wild cattle that different people had failed to get out when they gave up the lease. She told me that if I would give her my word that I would stay there until I got all the cattle out, she wouldn't charge me anything for the pasture; but I was to come to Austin after I had shipped out and give her a detailed report about the conditions of the grass and the fences and so on.

This sure was a relief to me, and I told her how much I appreciated it and that she could tell Barto Hood that I was capable of making trades without him. She laughed again and told me not to feel hard towards Barto, that he was a friend of both of us.

I wound up my visit pretty soon and was sayin' my good-byes when she handed me an envelope that was sealed and told me to give it to Eness when I got back to the ranch. I promised her I'd ride down and give it to him when I got back to the pasture.

Knowing I had plenty of time, I laid in a little more feed for my horses and a little more grub for myself and didn't work too hard at these cattle until Mustang's legs were about well and Beauty's withers had gone down to where a saddle didn't hurt her back. I had choused these cattle so much that they didn't run from me as bad in the thick brush, but they would hide and lay down and many times I guess I'd ride by them and never know they were there. Beauty could smell a steer and would stop or turn her head or ride toward them, which was a lot of help, and many an old-time brush cowboy will tell you that a brush cow horse sees and hears and smells more than the man riding it.

I had nineteen cattle in the small pasture the tenth day of December and got an old, wore-out cowboy to help me drive them to town and ship them. These were big cattle, but they weren't quite a carload. They brought $963 net after the freight and the commission was paid, which meant that if I could gather some more cattle out of that canyon, I'd begin to get paid for my work.

I'd learned all the cutoffs and bad trails and big rocks and logs by now, and was doin' a better job headin' these cattle off when they tried to get away. I was worryin' 'em more, but I wasn't catchin' 'em very fast! I rode by often and visited with Eness, and he didn't seem to be worried about my steers or about me and he often told me that everything was goin' to be "muy bueno," and I decided that his ideas of "muy bueno" and my ideas of "good" might be different.

Late in the afternoon on December 16 I rode by the

shack and took him a few little things that he had asked me to buy in town for him. There was a high northeast wind blowin'. There hadn't been any rain, the timber was dry, and these wild cattle, when you did see a few of 'em, you could tell they had begun to shrink 'cause the grass was gettin' short. This high windy afternoon Eness seemed to be in good spirits. He told me that if I was a good cowboy, like he thought I was, I would be up by daylight the next mornin' when the "norther" struck, that my wild cattle would drift from the wind and I would be able to get them out on the prairie. I told him that I didn't know how he knew so much about the weather and about the "norther" and that he might be able to read those steers' minds, but that I didn't think they had told him that they were goin' to go out on the prairie just because the wind blew.

He said, "My young friend, you have not much patience and have much to learn about wind and cattle."

I went back to camp, ate a big supper of beans, beef, and taters, and sour-dough bread. I left a horse in the small corral and just thought that I would take Eness's advice the next mornin'. Sure enough, along about midnight a norther struck. The wind was cold and I scuffled around and pulled some more saddle blankets on top of my bedroll. About four o'clock ole Beauty woke me up snortin' and whinnyin' and runnin' around the corral, and the other horses had run up to the corral and they were makin' a lot of horse noise. I rolled out of my bed and jerked my boots on and started dressin' as I walked out from under the shed. There was a big fire bein' fanned by a high wind comin' up the canyon from Eness's house towards the prairie, and cattle were bawlin' and runnin' ahead of the fire. The canyon was full of old wood and dead timber and cedar and other wood that would burn good since it was so very dry.

I saddled Beauty as fast as I could and rode into the clearing on the south side of the pasture and hazed and hollered and scared these cattle towards the corner where I had let the fence down two months before. By daylight all the cattle were out of the pasture and in the road driftin' and grazin' and bawlin' and startin' towards town. I turned my saddle horses out into the road with the cattle 'cause I knew that I might have to change horses several times before the drive was over that day.

By late afternoon I drove thirty-eight head of steers and two cows and calves and an old Mexican bull into the stock pens at the railroad, ready to ship. When I had the gates locked, I went up to the depot to order the cars to ship the cattle the next day. Then I rode uptown to the mercantile where I had been buyin' horse feed and supplies.

It was late afternoon and the old mercantile keeper said, "Would you like to see a note I have here?"

And at first it didn't make sense to me, and I said, "I don't remember signin' you a note."

"Oh Ben," he said, "Mrs. Marion signed this note and sent it to Eness by you."

Eness had been to town one time since I had been camped at the Marion pasture, and now I knew why—he had brought Mrs. Marion's letter to the old storekeeper so he could read it for him.

I picked the letter up off the counter; it read:

"Dear Friend Eness: I ask that you do a great favor for me and our young friend, Ben. When the wind and weather is right, fire the pasture as you did for Mr. Marion almost forty years ago. I know that Ben will do the rest and the Marion pasture will be free of wild cattle one more time."

STEERS

STEERS ARE A PRINCIPAL CLASS OF cattle that have long been referred to in livestock market quotations, various cattle operations, in song, stories, and legend. To my knowledge no writer has ever written the reason that bull calves are castrated and hence afterward known as steers, and due explanation has never been made as to their special purposes in the cattle industry.

In the early days of the cattle business in the Southwest there was little or no market for calves at weaning age except for the few ranchers who would buy them to keep on open range until they were older and bigger. The demand for "light" beef had not developed in the early-day consumer's trade as it has in modern times.

As bull calves develop into maturity, their shoulders and neck become thick and masculine with lots of cartilage and tissue developing in their muscle structure that is never palatable as human food unless it has gone through some grinding and other packer's processing. To keep a bunch of bull calves to develop into grown cattle running on one range amounted to a constant bullfight and not a profitable growth and flesh gain. By this brief explanation, the reader can readily understand that keeping a great herd of bulls was impractical and unprofitable.

When these bull calves are castrated, their growth pattern is changed and they do not produce coarse shoulders, thick necks, and other fleshing patterns that are undesirable for beef after they have reached a mature age. Great herds of steers can be run on open range or in fenced pasture in order that they may be grown into larger cattle without any particular difficulty of handling. This would show why it is most desirable from a cowman's standpoint to be raising steers.

It is common knowledge among stockmen that certain regions of semi-arid pasture land that is commonly referred to as rough—meaning mountains, rimrock, canyons that produce sparse, scattered vegetation—are more adaptable to beef production by the use of steers to graze such lands because steers can cover more ground to rustle for a living and gain weight than cows can and at the same time nurse a calf. This explains why there are vast semi-arid regions of the Western and Southwestern United States that are far more adaptable to steer beef-cattle operations than to those for cows and calves. At times of drouth or other adversity it is much easier to drive, ship, and relocate herds of steers than it is to move cows and calves.

A big steer in the early days of trail driving to Northern markets from the Southwest could make the trip on foot much faster than all other classes of cattle. He grazed along the way and maintained his flesh, and if he was driven across good grass country, might even gain weight on the trail drive. This is why "steer drives" are often referred to by cattlemen and historians of the past. The steer was the only class of cattle that could produce beef and transport itself to distant markets satisfactorily in the days when there were no railroads, trucks, and so forth. This factor alone would have caused him to be essential to a large beef-producing operation.

It is commonly known that steers were by far the best class of cattle to be used as oxen when they were put to the task of beast of burden. The steer's role in early agriculture and transportation has been written by historians to some extent, but the one great advantage of using steers on wagon trails for freighting purposes has been neglected.

All freighters liked mules best and horses second where trips were short enough to be made in three or four days since the amount of feed that had to be carried for horse and mule teams took up a considerable amount of space in the freight load. It was not advisable to use them on trips of more than several days because of this factor. However, steers could be used on long freighting trips or on long wagon-train trips by pioneers migrating to the West because they would be staked out at night to graze and, being animals of the Ruminantia family, they possess more than one stomach, and as they wear the yoke and pull the load, they belch up and chew this grass from the

night before and reswallow it back into the active diges-
tive track. This is the explanation omitted in history-book
accounts—that the steer had advantage over horses and
mules on long trips, just as long as he could get water and
graze at night. Extra feed in the form of grain did not
take up room on the freighter's load, and this, too, explains why, even though it took more time, it took less
money to freight with steers.

The steer was also much preferred in the pioneer
lumbering industry to haul logs or drag logs in the forest,
especially around the sawmill, because the split of his
cloven hoof gave him the advantage of pulling in soft
ground such as sand or mud without bogging down as a
horse does with a solid hoof that creates a vacumn each
time the horse drives it down into the mud and pulls it
out.

These are the principal reasons, then, that steers were
indispensable as beasts of burden in the development of
the West.

WILD,
WIDE-EYED
CATTLE

Tᴴᴱ ꜱᴛᴏᴄᴋ-ᴍᴀʀᴋᴇᴛ ᴄʀᴀꜱʜ ᴏꜰ ɪ9ᴢ9 had just stunned the world in general and upset the live-stock and commodities market along with the rest of the financial structure and economy of the world. Financiers were going broke and jumping out of windows and fore-

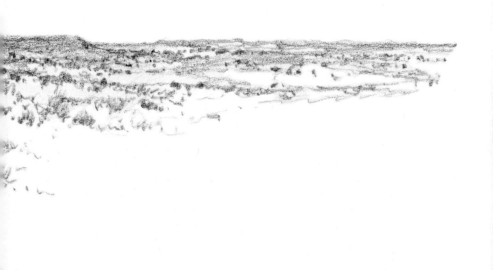

flushers were suddenly being flushed out and exposed as being penniless, and the cow business was the worst that I ever saw yet. I had some pastures leased (at too high a price) stocked with steers (that had cost too much) and apparently with no hopes of ever being able to pay out of debt, but there were a few factors in my favor. I was young, had ridden hard all my life, and even though I had made some money in the cow business, I had never taken time to spend any of it and when I made a profit had always just leased more land and bought more cattle, so whatever money that I had lost didn't impress me much because I hadn't sold the cattle and counted the money to realize how much was gone. Banks and loan companies were taking cattle and ranches and whatever else that they could grab in the financial disaster that had driven everybody to panic. Not being wise enough to know to worry, and having a complete disregard for cowards and weaklings and being sick of hearing people complain, I decided to go to a ranch that I had leased as far as I could get from town and hole up a while until loafing and visiting got to be a more pleasant pastime.

I was settin' on one end of the porch of my shack one afternoon and my favorite saddle horses were eatin' oats off the other end of the porch. A young cowboy keeps his horses as close to him as he can get 'em, and I don't guess I have lost the habit even this late in life. If I was building a place, I would still want a porch to feed my horses off of and lay on a pallet at night and listen to 'em eat, and I would want a water trough in the yard instead of a fish pond.

I was sittin' and coolin' and restin' and wasn't worrying too much about Wall Street when I saw a car come in past the gate about two miles up the hill. There was no mistake about it. Any time anybody came in that pasture gate, they were looking for me or they were lost because it sure wasn't no public road. Pretty soon this fella drove up and as I hollered to get out, he opened the door of his car and came through the yard gate, and it was natural for me to go to sizing him up. He was gray-headed, pale-complected, big-bellied, and was wearing a dress-up suit. He was wearing slippers and a white shirt, a bat-winged block bow tie, and had a little city kind of store hat on his head. You could tell for sure that if he had ever been a cowboy that he had got over it and was past riding age and had lost his shape for it.

We shook hands and he told me that he was Mr. Mc-Cloud, and you could just tell by the tone of his voice that he expected everybody to call him Mr. McCloud. You would get the impression from looking at him that he changed them white shirts every day, but from a cow-boy's point of view I don't know why, because he wasn't fixin' to do anything to get one dirty. We sat down on the edge of the porch and carried on a little worthless con-versation and pretty soon he came to the point. He was pasturing a bunch of big steers on the ranch east of my ranch, and the man who had been running the ranch and pasturing the cattle for him had gone broke and been took over by the bank, and he wanted to hire me to round up all, and he emphasized that word ALL, of his cattle for him and drive them to the railroad and ship them to Fort Worth. Money had suddenly gotten scarce and my spend-ing money was short and I decided that a little outside cow work wouldn't hurt me none, so we discussed how long it would take, how many cattle, and what he would pay me to get them to the railroad for him. Best he could figure, there were seventy-seven head of steers from three to five years old, branded with an open ʌ on the left jaw. I had seen these cattle a few at a time and knew that they were about half-breed Mexican and Hereford crosses and could be hard to handle. I didn't tell him so, but I felt like if I was lucky I might get them all out of that pasture in ten days. But I didn't want him to think that I was gettin' my money without ridin' for it, so I told him that I would deliver his steers *within* thirty days. I figured I would have to hire some extra help and mount them on my horses, and being out a little extra money for horse feed and grub I told him I would do the job for $100. This didn't seem to bother him a whole lot, so we made a trade and he went on back to Fort Worth, and I was to let him know when I was ready to load the cattle on the train. I sat there and laughed to myself about how easy it was to take a $100 away from a city fella that didn't want to ride after cattle. I told myself that I would just get two more cowboys—and cowboys were cheap and plentiful along about then—and make two big wide drives through that river bottom and canyon pasture and hand Mr. McCloud his cattle in a couple of stockcars.

This all happened along about middle of the week and I waited until about Saturday afternoon to ride into Granbury because I knew there would be some extra cowboys gathered in town on Saturday. I rode in and tied my horse to the chain around the courthouse and went over to Parks's Café to eat up a bunch of stuff and to get posted on how many ranchers the bank had took over and all the other sad news that old Parks would tell me in his broken tones. I was interested in puttin' out the word that I needed some cowboys because during the afternoon they would come in there to drink coffee.

I was driftin' around the square and had stopped over at Clyde Morris's hardware store, where there was always a bunch of men a-sittin' on some rolls of net wire. These were the days of prohibition and one of the best cowboys in the country was also the champion town drunk. He was a long, tall, whiskey-complected fella about twenty years older than me and a really good man to have on a cow drive. He walked up and tapped me on the shoulder and wanted to talk to me. We stepped back a piece from the rest of the loafers. His hands were shaky and he rubbed his face and said he heard I was needin' some help. I looked at him and could tell that he had been in pretty bad shape for days on that white lightnin' (corn whiskey), and I said, "Well, White Lightnin', my friend, I don't believe you are in shape to be of much help." He said he knew it and that was the reason that he wanted to get out of town for a while. So I told him what we had to do and if he wanted to work to meet me on the south side of the square about dark, and we would go to the ranch. Of course, he said he would be there but I wasn't countin' on him too big.

The word was gettin' around that I was lookin' for riders and it wasn't but a little while till another cowboy found me and he said he was fresh married and bad broke and sure did need to work. I told him I was paying $2 a day and we would batch in a camp and I would feed him and his horse, but I had plenty of my own horses for him to ride on the drive. This sounded good to him and he said that he would be ready to leave that afternoon but sure did need $5 to give his wife before we left town. I didn't know this boy too good but I let him have the $5 and sure enough we rode out that afternoon about dark and got into camp around ten or eleven o'clock and put our horses away and went to bed.

I got White Lightnin' full of some good hot breakfast and his nerves were settled considerably, and Newlywed was rarin' to go to work. It seemed like with just seventy-seven head of steers three men could ride out and come home with them in half a day. I hoped that was the way it would be, but I had seen these steers scattered around in the cedar breaks and up and down the river in the thickets and green briars and wild-grape vines and every-where else that it would be hard for a man on horse-back to follow a steer. I had a sneaking suspicion that no matter how many or how few cattle you had to get out of a pasture like this it could be trouble. We left the shack about sunup. It was Sunday mornin' but we was a way too far from church to disturb anybody and I didn't see any use in waitin' around a day or two to start earning that $100.

We surprised a bunch of these steers going up a can-yon headed out towards the open and by middle of the morning had forty head of them drifted up against the east outside fence. It was early in the day, and I couldn't see much use in trying to take them back to a set of holding pens so we stomped the barbed-wire fence down and pushed the cattle over the fence while we still had them in a driving mood; then we tied the fence back up behind us. If cattle intend to be bad, the sooner you can get them out of pasture they are used to, the sooner they point and drift the way you want them to go because they don't know where there is a thicket or a canyon to break back and get into. By late afternoon we had driven these cattle about eighteen miles and had them in the stock pens at Cresson, Texas, without any ordinary wild cow trouble.

Being Sunday, there wasn't any way for me to call Mr. McCloud at the telephone number he had given me, so Newlywed and White Lightnin' rode back to the ranch and I waited around in town until office hours Monday morning to call Mr. McCloud. I had to know where to ship these cattle and who to bill them to. Some nice-soundin' office gal answered the phone and said Mr. Mc-Cloud wouldn't be in for several days but had left instructions for the cattle to be shipped to T. Z. Ham Commission Company at the Fort Worth Stockyards, and that was what I was interested in finding out. So I got a stockcar and loaded the cattle and was back at the ranch in late afternoon. My cowboys had been eatin' and sleepin' and enjoyin' the rest.

Next morning we started out and rode into real trouble. These cattle were scattered three or four in a bunch all over the river bottom and the cedar breaks, and it didn't seem that they were on good terms with each other and were going to try to stay where they were. We rode, cussed, cried, whooped, hollered, and fought the brush and cedar thickets. When we came out to the top of the prairie about the same time and all three of us got up to where we could see each other, we had eleven head of cattle between us. These were big, old, rough, odd-colored red and brindled Mexican crossbreed cattle with no intentions of doing the right thing. There wasn't enough to ship and the hope of takin' them back to the canyon to the corral at my ranch was a lost cause because they would sure get away. I told Newlywed to ride way around them, let the fence down at the corner of the pasture which was about a mile ahead of us. As White Lightnin' and I held them in a pretty tight bunch and pushed them over the fence that Newlywed had let down, he asked me what I was going to do with them in that pasture knowing that it belonged to another rancher. I said, "It's a big open prairie pasture." I decided that I would just "pasture them out" until I got some more to go with them.

We rode hard all the rest of that week, and I had twenty-five in all pushed over in that prairie pasture by Saturday morning. One day we rode hard all day and didn't get a steer. The brush was thick and the vines were everywhere and the cedar was dense and these cattle had a good way to hide. Twenty-five wouldn't be a carload, but I was going to ship them anyway. We took them to Cresson by sundown and put them in the stock pens. When I told Newlywed and White Lightnin' that they could go back to the ranch and wait again until Monday for me until I shipped these cattle, they went to tellin' me a lot of things that I was already expecting. I had noticed that morning that both of them had got their own horse to ride on the day's drive instead of some of mine. White Lightnin's health had considerably improved on a good hard grub diet and hard work. He said he believed if I would pay him he would turn back to Granbury instead of going back to the ranch on Fall Creek. This wasn't no shock to me so I paid him, and about that time when Newlywed saw that I had money on me he spoke up and said he guessed he had better get back to Granbury too to see about his wife, so I paid him too. This left me without any help and twelve wild steers freshly boogered in a big canyon and river-bottom pasture. Since I already knew where these cattle were going, I billed them to T. Z. Ham Commission Company and loaded them Saturday night. I put my horse in the stock pens and fed and watered him and spent the night in the country hotel at Cresson.

Next morning I rode back to Weatherford to visit around and rest a day or two and let my wild cattle maybe settle down a little. I got to thinking that it would be a good idea to go over to Fort Worth and visit a little with Mr. McCloud and draw some of my money since I had delivered all of his steers but twelve. I went up to his office in the main part of Fort Worth and this lady that had been answerin' the phone told me that Mr. McCloud had not been back to the office yet and that she didn't know when to expect him. I looked around and I could tell that this was no cowman's office. He had big real-estate signs and pictures around on the walls with fancy furniture and rugs on the floor, and as I left I couldn't help but wonder about this Mr. McCloud.

I got on the streetcar and rode over to North Fort Worth to the stockyards, which was about five miles from the main part of Fort Worth. I went out on the stockyards and hunted up T. Z. Ham. He was a good honorable commission man; I had never had any business with him, but I knew him on sight and he knew me. This last twenty-five steers that I had shipped were in his sales pens. I shook hands and told him what I had been doing and that I had shipped him those steers for Mr. McCloud. He asked me if that would be all of them and I told him, no, that there was supposed to be twelve more head, but that I had found the carcass of one steer and there might be another one or two missing. Then I told him about going over to Mr. McCloud's office, and I also told him that McCloud owed me some money for gathering his cattle.

T.Z. said, "Let's go over here away from these other traders where we can talk." When we got back off in a corner of a steer pen, he said, "Ben, McCloud has skipped the country and don't nobody know where he is. I'm turn-ing the money from these cattle over to the bank and if anybody's going to pay you, it will have to be the bank. You better go talk to them while you're in town."

He gave me the name of the man to see in the bank, which was back over in the main part of Fort Worth. I went in the bank and sat around in one of them cold, hard-back mahogany chairs until somebody finally noticed me and asked me what I wanted. I told them who I wanted to see and pretty soon he came over to where I was sittin'. I got up and shook hands with him, and you could tell he wasn't very much of a banker. He was a little bitty fellow, narrow-eyed with a pair of thick glasses on and a little tight drawed mouth and with big ears and a squeaky voice. I told him what my business was and about the trade that I had made with Mr. McCloud to gather his cattle for $100. He was quick to tell me that the money for the forty head had been turned in and that Mr. Ham had called him that morning and told him about the twenty-five being on the day's market. We talked a few minutes, and I explained about the twelve head that would have to be got one at a time and tied and drug and fought to get to a corral and that it would take longer to get the twelve head than it had taken to get all the rest of them. He was quick to tell me how bad the cow market was and how little the steers was bringing and how much the bank was going to lose, and he guessed that the cattle that were left would be in awful bad shape by the time they would be hauled to the stockyards. I wasn't listening too careful and wasn't too much worried and thought I should still be entitled to draw $50 or $60 of the money. He explained to me further that the bank wasn't "bound" to live up the trades made by the defunct and now-missing Mr. McCloud and that he had just decided while we were talking that he would settle whatever was coming to me for my work by giving me the eleven head (one was dead) of cattle that were left in the pasture. If there was anything I didn't need it was some more cattle, but the way this Mr. "Narrow-eyed" Banker summed things up, it seemed like that was all I was going to wind up with for my work.

The steers that I didn't kill or cripple getting them out of that pasture were going to bring about three cents a pound and by the time they had been fought and drawed and drugged and hauled, they weren't going to weigh more than about 800 pounds, which would add up to more than $100 if and when I finally got them to where somebody could see them stand still long enough to bid on them.

When I got back to the ranch I packed in a good deal of grub, knowing that the moon might change several times before I caught eleven wild steers by myself. Up to now, I had been real lucky with my horses as none of them had gotten crippled or bad cut up or blemished by the brush in that river bottom. I had torn off a good many old clothes and lost a little hide myself, but my horses had been lucky and were standing the steer hunt maybe better than I was, and they didn't have to worry about whether I was going to get any money out of the trade.

A lone rider has to study the wind and try to ride with the wind against him to keep the cattle from knowing where he is, and the element of surprise every now and then pays off by helping you to sneak up close enough to get a throw with your rope at a wild steer. I played nearly all the tricks I knew and had caught five in eight days. When I did manage to tie on to one of these big wild steers, it was a good half day's work and sometimes longer to get him to the holding trap pasture that I had next to my camp. This little trap pasture had a seven-strand barbed-wire fence around it that had been built by somebody before me to be used to wean calves in after they had been cut off from the cows. I was putting it to good use but there was a small amount of land in the little pasture and if I didn't get the rest of the steers caught pretty soon, the steers that were in there were going to eat the grass up, which would make them more restless and they might try to break out.

These last four steers had worn me and my horses down and I thought I would ride over to Cleburne, which was about twenty-five miles away, just to take a little time to try to get some smart ideas. I was loafing around Scott's General Mercantile downtown close to the trade square when I heard a bunch of fellas talking about they're having considerable trouble finding a place to have a hound-dog trail. Well, I had never had time to *try* many hound dogs, so I stretched an ear out and listened real careful and it seemed their problem was that nobody wanted all the noise and commotion of the gathering of the men and dogs before they started a wolf hunt, and none of the ranchers felt like they caught enough wolves to go to the trouble of rebuilding the fences they tore down and cleaning up the camp and finding all the dogs they lost.

That wasn't really what they were saying, but that was what it added up to to me. I spoke up and kinda made myself known and said I would like to see a good two- or three-day wolf hunt, and I felt like there were plenty of wolves in the pasture that I had in mind. Seemed like the ringleader was an old man with a pair of suspenders and a big chew of tobacco, and he got to quizzing me as to where I was talking about for this wolf hunt. I explained to him that some of them could camp on the river and others could camp on the prairie when the moon and weather was just right. They could turn one big pack of dogs loose to run down the canyon and another big big pack of dogs loose to run the river and that they were sure to flush out enough wolves to try their dogs and make the hunt worth-while. It was late summer and getting a little fallish at night and these fellas set a time about four days from then as when they would all gather. I drew them some maps on a brown-paper sack and explained to them how to come and where to camp and said that I'd sure be looking for them.

I got a shave and a haircut, ate some town grub, bought a few little things I needed, and headed back to the ranch pretty early in the afternoon. I just tried to remember—it didn't seem like I'd ever seen a wolf in that part of the country or any wolf signs, but it sure was going to be interesting to see if fifty or sixty dogs and that many hunters would have any nerve-rackin' effect on them big steers that was so snug in that underbrush along that river bottom and hidden in those cedar breaks up and down the canyon in that pasture. I felt like the old boys would have a nice camping place and a big visit and exercise their dogs and my steers whether they exercised any wolves or not.

Sure enough, along middle of the evening on the day they were supposed to be there, they began to gather with all colors and shapes and sizes of hounds. They set up their two different camping places and built fires and laughed and hollered and talked and carried on the kind of commotion that would carry good on the wind and make them big steers turn restless. I rode up to each camp a little before dark and explained to them the way I felt they would do the most good with the hounds, and I told them that I wouldn't be able to be with them but to have a good time and leave the next day when they got ready. There had been a light shower a day or two before where it was just right for a dog to be able to trail, and the moon was full and came up early. In the early part of the night I heard them turning their dogs loose. I could hear them barkin', bayin', bawlin', yippin', and carryin' on, making all kinds of dog noise. They were starting their hunt just the opposite direction from which I had been trying to hunt cattle, and if my strategy worked they were going to booger those big steers right along down the canyon against the fence line, which was a fair-size pasture that joined the little holding trap.

I had already spent the afternoon taking wire loose and tying it to the bottom of the post at four different places on the fence line and had opened the plank gate that joined the two pastures, and at the far-northwest end I had let the fence down in the corner. When I left the last dog camp just at dark, I had turned my horse and rode to a high ridge farthest from where the hunters would start and at a point where I could see the fence line in three or four places if the moon was right. The dogs had been running and circling and tryin' to pick up a scent for a good while. About midnight I saw the brush rattle down on the flat below me and three big steers broke out of the cedar breaks, wringing their tails, their heads up, looking for new country.

During all the hard ridin' that I had done I had found the carcasses of two more steers, which meant that there were only nine in all, and this was cuttin' down on the amount of money that I might finally get. So according to this count there was just one more steer in the pasture that the dogs hadn't flushed out. I watched these three steers as they headed towards the fence on the west side of the pasture; they were looking for a hole to go through. They went behind a clump of trees and out of sight. I heard one of them bawl. The next time I saw them they were about a quarter of a mile over in my pasture and you could see their outlines in the moonlight; they acted like they had smelled the cattle in the trap and were moving that way. I waited a little while to see the other steer but my nerves couldn't stand it any more, so I rode the fence line and let the wire back up in the places I had tied it down and tied it back to the post and started to my camp. I thought these old steers were boogered pretty good, and even though wild cattle drive a little better in the moonlight because they don't quite see a rider so good, I didn't dare push my luck. I eased on to camp and let my horse stay in the yard and eat off the porch, and I had my saddle and rigging laying handy 'cause I would want to use it about daylight.

I never knew how many wolves those fellas caught, but that other steer had managed to come in during the night and was with those three steers, hanging along the fence where I had the other steers. I opened the gate to the trap pasture knowing that I might spill the ones I had caught, but it was a chance I had to take. I rode way wide around these last four and it seemed to me like it took them a long time to drift up close to that gate, but they finally did go through the gate and I rode up right easy and closed it behind them. I knew all the time that Mr. Banker never thought that I would gather enough of those cattle to barely pay me for my trouble, and I felt pretty smart about having them in that small trap pasture.

Trucks weren't very big in those days and a bobtail truck would hold about five head of cattle, but there was no road that a truck could come in on down to this little pasture, and if you could get a truck in there was a good corral but no loadin' chutes or crowding pens. My troubles weren't over because I still had to drive those cattle out of that canyon and through another man's pasture out to the public road. I let my horses rest and worried about this for two or three days.

I didn't want to take the chance of having some loud-mouthed cowboy come help me that might holler at the wrong time and scatter these steers back to the brush. The grass was shorter in the little trap and pretty soon all I was going to have there would be plenty of water and too many steers. There were two corrals that I could put these cattle in. I could put the steers in one corral and cut one at a time into the other corral that had a big, heavy *bois d'arc* snubbin' post in the center of the corral which was set about five feet in the ground and had been there a long time. (A snubbin' post is used when you rope bronc horses or bad cattle and need to draw them up tight in order to do something to them.)

I was ridin' a big light chestnut horse called Dan. We cut about the biggest and rankest brindle-colored steer into the pen where the snubbin' post was and I roped him around the horns. (If a steer is roped around the neck he will choke and that will make him fight a lot more.) He turned and charged Dan, and as Dan dodged the steer we made a jump toward the snubbin' post, and I took a wrap around the snubbin' post and drew this steer up to it until his head was solid against the post with a horn on each side. Dan was a big stout horse and I intended for him to hold the steer while I worked on him.

The last time I was in town a bunch of us cowboys was sittin' around talkin' about wild steers and one smart-aleck old cowboy jokingly said that if there's some way to prop a steer's eyes open, he wouldn't run into the brush if he couldn't close his eyes. Since I had been wondering how I was going to get these cattle out of that brush canyon, that bright batch of conversation had worried me considerably. It's common knowledge that the reason bullfighters stay alive is that the bull shuts his eyes when he makes that last lunge off the ground to charge a bullfighter. Even a man won't run into brush without turning his arm up to protect his head and eyes.

I had spent the night before cuttin' and sharpenin' some green live-oak pegs about as big around as a pencil and about two to three inches long and some even longer. I had never done this and I didn't know what length peg it would take to hold a steer's eyelids open. I stepped off of Dan, and he knew how to set back on that rope with his head to the steer to keep the steer's head pulled up against that post. I took my pocketknife and lifted the upper lid of one eye and punctured a hole through to the outside, and I intended to puncture a hole in the lower eyelid and put the sharpened ends of the live-oak pegs in the holes that I was cuttin', which would "prop" the steer's eyes open. I had really forgotten that old Dan was a little bit "flanky." When that steer went to bawlin' and pullin' as hard as he could with just one wrap of that rope around that snubbin' post, the pressure got pretty bad on that back cinch and Dan, instead of pullin', humped up and jumped forward, which gave the steer plenty of slack to rake me with his horns as I barely got out of the way. The last jump Dan made gave the steer enough slack so that he had more length of rope from the post than Dan had. He raked old Dan down the side with one horn and got the blood in a place or two, then hit him in the chest and punctured a hole that brought Dan back to his senses. It was common horse sense that that cinch wasn't as ticklish as the damage that steer was giving him, so he snorted, backed his ears, turned, and pulled that steer's head back up to the snubbin' post.

While Dan was takin' lessons from that steer I took some too. I knew that this snubbin'-post business was going to be too risky for me to get all those steers' eyes propped open. Cowboys don't like footwork, post-hole diggin', or using an ax, but it looked like I had my business in such a shape that I was going to have to think about doing some hard common labor. I cut a lot of good cedar poles, straight and about eight feet long, built me a small crowding pen in the corner of the big corral with a short chute that would hold two big steers at a time. I built the front of the chute solid, with no chute gate to let them out at, and the back of the chute was where you could block them with cedar poles crosswise and then back them out of the chute when you were through with them. Between cuttin' poles and draggin' them out of the canyon horseback, all this took me little over a week. The cattle weren't getting any gentler in that time but they were gettin' more used to seein' a man and weren't spooking quite as bad when I rode past the fence draggin' a few poles with a saddle horn.

Early one morning I worked around as slow and quiet

as I could and got this nine head in the corral. I threw a slicker over the gate I brought them in at, so that they would be scared enough that they wouldn't try to go back out that gate. These old steers were sure rank. They would fight a man afoot and they would fight you horseback, and it took a lot of dodgin', jumpin', and climbin' fences to keep your good health. I finally got two of them in the crowding pen in the chute and blocked to where they couldn't get out, and then I started the work of preparing these cattle's attitude for driving without trying to get away and run into the brush.

I put a rope on the first steer and pulled it up against the post and corral fence on the fence side of the crowding chute. He bawled, fought, bellowed, and let out the alarm. I slit a small place from inside on his upper eyelid and then inside on the lower eyelid. I took one of those green live-oak pegs that I had sharpened on each end and stuck the ends through each slit I had made with my pocketknife and propped the steer's eyelids open. The pegs had to be long enough to stretch the eyelids to where the pressure would hold them in place. The pegs didn't touch the eyeball, and I wasn't worried too much about the little dab of blood or the pain caused the steers 'cause any one of them would have horned me and my horse and killed us in a minute if he had gotten the chance. It was almost dark when I finished pegging the eyelids of the last steer, but it was a sight how gentle it made them. They looked at me and looked at my horse, but they never made another run at either of us.

The next morning I turned these cattle out by myself and rode along behind them and winged them from one side to the other and drove them up a trail past my shack and turned them toward the trail that finally would lead out to the public road. I have drifted milk cows and pet horses and mules and all other classes of livestock across all kinds of country, but no animals have ever walked in the middle of a trail as far away from a swinging limb or bush as these steers did. I guess the pegs that crossed their eyeballs looked about the size of telephone poles, and after they had been in there overnight, I am sure their eyelids might have been a little sore.

I drove my nine head of cattle out of the brush up the road past Cresson and on to Weatherford in two days, and after I had them in a good set of loading chutes I flipped the pegs out of their eyelids and put the steers in trucks and sent them to the Fort Worth market. By now they weighed less than 800 pounds apiece and after the hauling and commission was paid netted me $21 a head, which came to $189. I had paid Newlywed and White Lightnin' $16 each, which left me with $57 more than Mr. Banker would have owed me if he had paid me the $100, and at this time this was a big lot of money for a month's work.

BLACK HEIFERS CROWHOP

JOE BARWISE IN FORT WORTH WAS AT-
torney for the Fort Worth and Denver Railroad and a few
other major operators in Texas but his clientele was very
limited. I was just a wild rough young cowboy, but Judge
Barwise and I had had several livestock deals and our

dealings had always been pleasant and profitable and I suppose this was the reason that he was callin' me long-distance. Along about this time you only got a long-distance call when it was a sure-enough must.

Charlie Sharp stepped out of his grocery store on the corner of the square to holler at me that Fort Worth was callin' me long-distance. I rode up and dropped the reins on my horse (which is tyin' a horse Texas-fashion) and went into the grocery. This was one of my several loafin' spots and the local telephone operator knew that it would be one of the places where she might find me. Pretty soon Charlie got the operator and Judge Barwise asked me how soon I could come to Fort Worth. I knew that there would be a Red Ball bus just about noon and he told me to be on it if I wanted to make a good cow deal with him and the railroad.

I went to his office in Fort Worth and he was walkin' the floor and a-waitin' for me. There had been a small train accident up close to Bowie on the Fort Worth and Denver Railroad and a carload of forty head of black two-year-old heifers had been crippled or killed or turned loose. The best count that he had from the claim agent was that there was twenty-three alive and runnin' loose on the vegetable farms, orchards, cornfields, and oat patches somewhere a few miles east of Bowie.

After he had painted the picture and told me his trouble, he asked me what I would give, range delivery, for twenty-three head of two-year-old Black Angus-and-Brahma-crossed heifers. I told him that I needed to use his phone and talk to the stockyards. According to his and the claim agent's information, Gib Wright had bought and sold the heifers. Gib already knew about the train wreck and he told me that the heifers would bring $26 and a few cents at the rate of five cents a pound. I hung up the phone and told Judge Barwise that it was a two and a half or three days' ride on horseback from Weatherford to the place where the heifers were supposed to be and they would probably have to be caught one in a bunch, and I painted the story about as bad as I guess it really was and offered him $10 a head.

The Judge gave me a nice gentleman's argument that would have sounded good before a jury about how little trouble it would be to catch these heifers, and how the railroad couldn't afford to lose that much money, and how to take the price that I had offered him would be ridiculous.

I said, "Judge, in view of your analysis of the heifer situation, why don't you just have the section crew catch 'em by hand and lead 'em back to town."

He bowed up at me and looked over his glasses, cleared his throat, and said, "Ben, that's ridiculous!"

I answered, "I was just tryin' to even up the ridiculous score in this conversation."

I got up about like I was about to leave and he said, "Where have you started for?"

I said, "Well, nowhere in particular, but anywhere that I would be goin' I'd be doin' more good than I'd be doin' here arguin' with you about a bunch of wild heifers three counties away that you never even saw, and I never even saw, and you suggestin' that I pay money for them!"

"Well," he said, "I'm just trying to represent the interest of the railroad, and I didn't intend to be trying to take advantage of you." And, as an afterthought, he added, "I don't think I need to worry about that, so maybe you better pay me for the heifers."

I said, "I'll give you a check for fifteen head and then pay you by the head for any more that I gather above that number."

He said that would be all right because he knew I would finally catch them all.

With this batch of business tended to, I caught a bus later in the afternoon and went back home and rode off next morning with four good horses and a pack to go gather my black heifers out of the orchards and fields of the farmers that were pasturin' 'em involuntarily.

The third day I found the place on the railroad right of way where the car had turned over and the cattle had gotten away. Of course, the railroad had been repaired in a matter of hours and the only signs were a few dead cattle and some new ties and rails. I found a creek with water in it close to the spot and lots of tall grass up and down the railroad right of way. It was late and I made camp and studied about my heifers till morning.

I rode toward Bowie the next morning and asked along the way about the heifers and everybody had something to tell me. Some of the folks were real nice and hoped I could catch them and told me to ride through their fields and pastures and do whatever I had to to get the heifers off of their land. Of course, there were a few that were hateful and wanted to know who they could sue for the watermelon or whatever else had been damaged and hoped that the railroad price for the stuff might be better than the town price.

I was fast to catch on, and that I had better explain that I wasn't in any position to be doin' any settlin' or payin' off for the railroad and the most help that I could be would be to get the stock off the land to where they wouldn't do any more damage. I had gathered all kinds of wild stock and strays and I knew the Texas Stray Law. It had been written in the days of big ranches and was phrased to discourage farmers and nesters from unnecessarily penning livestock for damages.

In my conversation with those people that were a little huffy, I always explain that the one way that they could get some money for their damages was to pen the heifers that were runnin' on them and have the sheriff or constable advertise them as strays. *I knew* that the law required that the animals strayed be confined in a pen, fed, watered, and properly cared for for a full twenty days before the sheriff or constable could sell them at auction. Then the man holding the strays could bid his amount of damages and was allowed ten cents per head per day for care for the number of days that he had them penned up. So I encouraged these farmers who were mad to pen all these heifers they could and "stray" them, since the owner, under the law, could claim them and pay the ten cents per head per day as soon as they were posted by law as strayed and didn't have to wait the full twenty days.

Of course I could have argued with them about the damages and I sure would have been glad to pay the thirty or forty cents per head due for these heifers penned and kept a few days instead of me havin' to ride after them, but none of these "pumpkin rollers" fell for that story because they knew they couldn't catch them and, besides, none of them had a pen or corral of any sort that would hold these little jumpin' crow-lookin' black heifers.

This would probably no longer be the case since the Texas Stray Law was rewritten about 1960 to state that anyone caring for a stray animal is entitled to $1 per head per day for care.

I knew now why Judge Barwise wanted to sell me the heifers. His greatest fear was not for the value of the heifers but for all the damages that the railroad might be gettin' into from the farmers whose land the heifers were runnin' wild on. Well, this kind of conversation set pretty well with them.

By noon I had found the schoolhouse. It was summer and school was out, and of course the grass was growed up big around the schoolhouse. There was a water well with a hand pump on it. The schoolhouse was fenced around on three sides and open on the front toward the road, and it seemed like this would be a real good campground for me and my horses. I unsaddled my pack horse in the shade of a big tree on the back side of the school grounds plumb out of sight of the road. I staked my extra horses with long stake ropes, and I decided I would try to make acquaintance with some of my heifers between then and sundown.

I rode to the northwest across a field whose owner had said that some heifers had gone through and might be on the headwaters of Denton Creek, which ran behind his house. Well, that water up Denton Creek wouldn't amount to much in the way of a stream but would have some grazin' on it. Sure enough, I found three heifers standin' in the shade and when I got within hearin' distance, they threw up their heads and those big floppy ears came forward, and though they couldn't see me I knew they could smell and hear my horse. (Some people may not know that cattle can't see as far as horses or as men, but they can smell a long way farther than they can see if the wind is in the right direction, and then they go to tryin' to hear what they smell.)

I reined my horse to the west of them, thinkin' maybe I could get a little closer to them, but directly they bounced out from under that tree and the three heifers went three or four different directions. I saw quick that they weren't goin' to herd and drive, so I decided I had better have one of them than none at all.

I took after what looked like the slowest one, and just before she dived into the thicket I set the loop of my rope down at the bottom of her horns and turned, and ole Beauty stuck her feet in the ground and turned that heifer a big nerve-rackin' flip. There wasn't a whole lot of fight in these heifers. They were too young for that, but their experience with stockcars and railroads had had a bad effect on their dispositions and they sure would try to get away. I drove and jerked and maneuvered and pulled this heifer back to my camp just before dark. I staked her to a nice gentle tree and she bawled and fought that rope and threw herself down a good many times before she quit fightin'.

As I fixed me some supper and fed my horses, I worried about what I was goin' to do with these heifers after I caught them. I couldn't stake them to a tree and let them stand there a week or two waitin' to catch the rest of them, and none of these farmer people had cow lots or corrals that would hold wild cattle. After me and the horses had finished with supper, I pumped water from the school well and watered everything except that heifer.

Next morning she was standing astraddle of the rope pullin' out away from the tree with her head about half-way to the ground, and I just thought all these heifers have jumped several fences and will jump some more, and if I could just tie her head down to about the position she had it in now she couldn't do anything but graze. Any four-legged animal, be it horse, cow, or deer, has to be able to raise its head in the effort and motion of raising its forelegs before it can jump, so I just took me a short rope and tied it around that heifer's horns underneath my lariat rope where I could get it up later.

While she pitched I managed to get the head rope pulled down and tied in a bowline knot—so it wouldn't get any tighter—just under her ankle and above her foot around the pastern joint with her head drawn down about four inches lower than the level of her back. I eased around and untied the lariat rope from the tree, and with that one foot to where she would jerk it off the ground with her head, I could very easily hold her with me on the ground afoot until I could get a hold of the lariat rope and jerk it off her horns. She thought she was loose and made two or three wild jumps to leave, each time trippin' and throwin' herself. After a while she stood there mad and thoroughly disgusted with me and the rest of the human race, but in spite of this she had her mouth in reach of grass and water.

In a week's time I had four or five miles of the public road stocked with black heifers with their heads tied to their foot and had become the talk of the community. Everybody was friendly and tellin' me where they saw the last one of my heifers. I had been changin' horses twice a day and rode hard and had twelve head gathered.

During this time I had visited everybody out of the notion of suing the railroad without ever tellin' them that I had bought the cattle and the railroad didn't really have anything to do with them. I had eaten watermelon during the daytime when I was ridin' through the fields and visited with the people who had gardens, fresh roastin' ears, peaches that were ripe, and fryin' chickens that were plentiful. I don't believe I ever fattened on a cow-workin' as much as I did on this one. Folks who stay at home and raise stuff are nice to know, especially when you are gatherin' wild cattle off their land for them.

I had pretty thoroughly determined that there were eleven more heifers and that the twenty-three count was right. There were two heifers back in a big pasture about six miles from the road that I was leavin' for last. Every afternoon I would ride up and down the public road and herd my crowhoppin' heifers to where the creek ran for a drink and drive them into the school grounds to bed up for the night.

The stock laws and speed limits were different in those days. There was little or no danger of anybody drivin' fast enough to hit a heifer and, besides, at that time the man drivin' the car was liable for damage to livestock, instead of the other way around, as the law is today; if livestock that are on a public road are hit by a car, the owner of the livestock is liable for both the damage to the vehicle and any injury to the driver.

I had finally worked my heifer herd into the public road where they could graze along the right of way. I had to go into Bowie to buy some extra rope, but I had the heifers grazin' and drinkin' and fillin' up with their heads down and not jumpin' any more fences.

The time had come for me to go after the two heifers that were farthest from the road and in the biggest pasture. They had been loose the longest and I didn't know whether that had caused them to settle down and get over some of their fright or whether it had caused them to be wilder. I threw a mess of cooked meat, bread, onions, and stuff in a brown-paper sack and rolled it up in my jumper and tied it on the back of my saddle, countin' on this being an all-day ride, and took Beauty for my day's mount. The pasture that I had heard my heifers were in was probably a thousand acres and kinda rough with a creek runnin' through the middle of it, which meant that the two heifers could water 'most anywhere and there wasn't any certain spot that I could wait to trap them.

During all this heifer-catchin', I had been takin' the wire loose on these old, sorry fences and tyin' it to the bottom of the post in one place until I rode over and then let the wire back up and tied them. I always carried a strand or two of baling wire wadded up pretty short and wrapped to the back cinch ring of my saddle.

I was in this pasture by good sunup, hopin' to have some luck catchin' one or both of these heifers before the day got too hot. The creek ran east and west through the pasture and the brush wasn't too dense. You could ride by a thicket or at least ride around it and see all the way through it, but at this hour of the morning I thought these heifers ought to be out in an open glade or on a ridge grazin'.

In a short while I spotted a small herd of various shades of red-and-yellow-colored cattle grazin' on a slope with two sure-enough black heifers among them, and I knew from the size and shape and hair that these were my last two heifers. Knowin' that this must be a herd of gentle cows and calves, I whistled and sang and made a little noise and came in pretty close range with them, hopin' to get a quick throw at a black heifer and maybe not disturb the rest of the bunch too much. This was bad thinkin' because, as soon as I got out of the brush and in good view, the two black heifers left the bunch and started for the brush along the creek.

Since I had roped every heifer I had caught, I didn't think there was any use hopin' for better now, so I took down my ropes and fastened one of them to Beauty's saddle horn almost in a matter of minutes. Each heifer that I roped had offered to fight a little when I got off my horse and went to put the head rope on her that I was goin' to tie to her foot, and I learned early to maneuver around and let the heifer think she was gettin' away until I got her to some sizable tree or sapplin'; then I would run around the tree, and when I had one or two wraps around the tree with my rope, I would back my horse up and take the slack out until I had her head pulled up within three or four feet of the tree. This way I could get off my horse and go to the heifer without her being able to meet me on the way and start a fight, and by havin' her rope wrapped around that tree, it took a lot of pull off my horse. You can throw at a heifer's horns or neck or maybe rope a forefoot when she only has three or four feet of rope to play on without much danger. So I got this heifer to wind herself around a fair-sized tree that was standing in the opening, and I took one of the head ropes that I carried tied on the back of my saddle with the same saddle strings that I tied my jumper with.

It didn't take but a few minutes to get a rope on her head and down to her foot and tie it in a bowline knot with what little slack she had between her and the tree. I had two extra lariat ropes with me and I decided to leave her tied to that tree just in case I wanted to yoke the other one to her and make them drive and handle a little better. I stepped back on my horse and looked around; there wasn't a cow brute to be seen.

I rode the ridge and the valley across the creek several times the rest of the morning, and about late afternoon, when cattle would normally come out from shadin' up to graze, I found this same little herd of cattle at the far end of the pasture and the black heifer had rejoined them. This heifer was a little bigger than the average of them, and maybe a little wilder. The wind was against me and the cattle hadn't smelled me, so I rode in pretty close with my rope ready and easin' along until the heifer made the first move and started the race.

She was not only a little bigger, she was a little faster too, and we had to take her a long ways before she began to wind enough for Beauty to put me close enough to rope her. I was never the best roper in the world and in this modern-day times of rodeo'n' probably wouldn't have been able to win a dollar, but I was always steady enough to catch enough stock to make a livin' horseback. I set that rope on my last black heifer. When Beauty stopped we didn't flip this one into the air. The heifer pulled hard and turned and started back to us, and when we dodged her that time, sure enough, we did throw her hard enough to knock the wind out of her. She got up like she was leavin', and we gave her slack and followed and drove her back towards the first heifer that I tied that morning.

She wrapped herself around a small sapplin' a little before I was ready for her to, but I took the hint and went to gettin' down and slipped my head rope off the saddle to go to her. This sapplin' was pretty limber and from her pullin' on it one way and Beauty pullin' the other, the wrap bent the sapplin' and the rope slipped off and I guess I had gotten a little careless by now, and this heifer hit me a good hard lick in the ribs and I heard something pop that I was pretty sure wasn't her skull, but I didn't take any time out. She turned to come back and fight me, and instead of tryin' to put a rope on her head, I just looped the rope on her forefoot and jerked it out from under her and, while she was down, tied it up to her head. I got back on my horse and worked her on up to the tree where the other heifer was and without too much trouble got them yoked together.

It was gettin' real late and I knew that I wouldn't have daylight enough to get through the fences and back to the school grounds with this pair before dark. Just over the west fence line of this pasture was an oat field in the creek valley. The oats had been cut and bundled with a binder and shocked in stacks of about ten to twelve bundles to cure in the air and sunlight before the harvest would be finished by thrashin' the oats. This is all done now with a combine and you never see oat shocks any more. I rode up to a big live-oak tree on the fence line and unsaddled Beauty, crawled through the fence, and pitched her about three big bundles of oats. Of course, Beauty had been fed everything from cream of wheat to chicken feed and she knew how to bite the oat heads off those bundles.

By this time I began to get my breath a little short and the place where I got that lick in my side had begun to sore up and throb a little bit. I took the rest of that shock of oats and laid the bundle under the shade of that big tree in about the shape of a pallet, laid the heads of the bundles to the inside from both sides, which made a soft place up and down the middle, and unfolded my saddle blanket and spread it across the top of my oat-bundle pallet. It was almost dark and I had my heifers tied, my horse fed, and my bed made, and I left ole Beauty untied so she could go to the creek to water; I knew she would come to call next morning. I ate what I had saved from my noonday lunch and stretched out for the night.

I waked up early and, after I did manage to struggle around and stand up, decided I was goin' to live. I had ribs broken before, so I knew what my ailment was, but I hadn't quite figured out how many were broken until I picked up my saddle and started to throw it on my horse in the usual manner. This damn near took my breath.

Me and Beauty took the two heifers back to the school grounds and I rested that afternoon and never did unyoke this last pair of heifers. The next morning I broke camp, put my pack on one of my horses, and turned the other two in the road with my crowhoppin', head-down black heifers and drove them into Bowie and waved goodbye to my farmer friends that lived along the road. I loaded my cattle late that afternoon at Bowie, put my saddle horses in the other end of the car (there was plenty of room), and rode the caboose into Fort Worth.

The next morning we put my heifers in a chute in the stockyards and took all the ropes off and drove them down to the commission firm's sellin' yards to be sold that day. I got on the streetcar and went over to big-town Fort Worth and paid Judge Barwise for the other eight heifers.

When I finished the deal and started home with my horses, I wasn't much richer or much older, but I was wiser in that I knew how to tie a cow brute's head to her forefoot after I had a tree between her and my horse.

FRIENDLY—?
COW TRADE

ONE NICE, BALMY SPRING DAY LESter Lewis, who was a jackpot cow trader and a good friend of mine, came up the road followin' a small bunch of mixed farmer-type of cattle, Jerseys and crossbreeds. He was grazin' them along the road. When he got even with the ranch gate, he rode inside and I looked out and hollered at him to get down and come in. We would have dinner ready in a little bit. Me and some more boys were batchin' takin' care of a bunch of steers and we all took time about cookin' and this happened to be one of the days I wasn't cookin'.

Lester came in and we had our howdy's around and sat on the edge of the porch just outside of the kitchen visitin', when Dave asked Lester if he had any milk cows in that bunch that was givin' milk. Lester said he had a good cow that was givin' plenty of milk. So Dave up and says, "Ben, why don't you trade for us a milk cow?" Well, I never drink milk and hadn't felt like I had been doin' without anything good, and I sure wasn't goin' to milk a cow—I felt like that was "woman's work." Me and the boys jawed back and forth and they agreed that they would milk the cow and take care of the milk if I would trade for a milk cow.

Dinner wasn't quite ready so Lester and I walked out among his cows, that had stopped along the road and were grazin'. The cow he showed me was a nice, dish-faced, crumpled-horn, beautiful small Jersey cow with a great big udder. Lester said he didn't get the calf with her and didn't know how long she had been milking, but said she gave so much milk that he had to milk her out this morning on the road. I asked him why would a man trade off that good a milk cow. He said the fellow that he got her from told him that she was suckin' a cow of his, and he said, "I know it's so because since I've had her she has sucked a cow of mine."

I let out a big horse laugh and said that wouldn't be

no problem on this ranch because I didn't have anything but steers and he thought that was kinda funny and laughed too.

I traded him a good two-year-old halter-broke young horse even for the cow, which wasn't a bad trade for either one of us. We turned the cow into a small trap pasture by the house and tied the young horse to the gatepost so Lester could lead him when he started to drive his cows up the road.

We was all sittin' around the table eatin' a big batchin' dinner of beef, beans, and taters, and I was sittin' on the side facin' out the window. Everybody was nearly finished eatin' when I looked out the window and said, "That damn cow is suckin' herself."

Lester said, "Yep, she's suckin' your cow now."

PICTURESQUE STEERS

ONE JULY MORNING I WAS IN THE Fort Worth Stockyards upon "the high bridge," which was an overpass over the railroad tracks that went through the stockyards for footbackers, and when you wanted to find somebody you got upon the high bridge and looked

for them. I wasn't exactly huntin' anybody, I was just killin' time, when a nicely dressed uncowman-lookin' fellow stopped and said, "I hear you buy cattle, range delivery, and catch them yourself."

I said, "I have been known to do that foolish a stunt, but I'm not as anxious now for that kind of trade as I used to be."

Well, he introduced himself by that time, and he was from some land and cattle company in Chicago and they had foreclosed a ranch on some poor cowboy out in Borden County. He thought he had eight big steers in a three-section pasture that he would like to sell me, and he talked on to tell who all had seen these steers, and he was sure there were eight of them and didn't suppose they would be any trouble to get. It was just that he was from Chicago and didn't have much of any way to get to these cattle himself.

Of course, I could tell by the way he was dressed, the tone of voice he was usin', and the way his fingernails was manicured that he could have done just as much about these cattle in Chicago as he would be· able to in the pasture with them.

He talked on a little and I got a good idea of the direction where this pasture was, and I knew that it was a good two hundred miles or more from Fort Worth, and it would be a good deal of trouble to get me and my horses out there, and after I got eight head of steers, what I would do with them? There wouldn't be enough to ship and I would have to sell them at Snyder or Sweetwater or somewhere to another cow buyer, and I told him all this and told him that maybe he ought to get him somebody

closer to the cattle to buy 'em. He countered this proposition by tellin' me that he was on his way back to Chicago
and that he wasn't going to make a trip back out to
Borden County to sell eight head of steers.

By now, I had made it pretty plain that it wasn't a
very good proposition for me, so I finally asked him what
he would take for these steers. I didn't think it was any
use in askin' him how big they were or what they would
weigh or how old they were, 'cause I didn't figure he
would have enough sense to know anyway. He asked me
if I would give $400 for all of them, and I said, "No, much
obliged. That might be all they are worth when they are in
the stockyards."

He talked roundabout what stock were bringin'—six
and seven cents a pound—and that these cattle would
surely be worth twice that much, so I said, "To show you
how far apart we are, I figure I would give you half that
much, which would be $200."

He had a pair of fancy gloves in his hand and he
twisted them up in a tight wad and looked over the
stockyard, kinda bit his lip like a nervous woman, and
said, "Well, if that's as much as you will give for them, I
think I will sell them to you, range delivery."

I started to pay him out of my pocket and he said,
"No, let's go to the office of John Clay Commission Company, and I will give you a bill of sale for them and then
you can pay me."

Well, that was gettin' proper for just a common trade
of eight head of steers, but I didn't exactly know how
they done cow business in Chicago, so we went to John
Clay Commission office in the Exchange Building and fin-

ished the deal. After I had handed him the money and he had handed me the bill of sale that I didn't ask for, he sets in with a long legal rigamarole about these being my cattle and from here on I would be responsible for anybody they injured or any damage they did, and he went on and on, and from what he said, you would have thought these cattle was in the middle of a flower garden surrounded by little children in downtown Fort Worth. I knew there were so few people in Borden County in those days that all that conversation that he put out forewarnin' me was wasted.

I spent the rest of the day up and down the stockyards for no particular reason except to stay in the shade of the different commission offices and stand around the Exchange Building where them big ceiling fans was a-stirrin' up the hot air.

That night I went over to the main part of Fort Worth and was eatin' supper in the Texas Hotel. Of course, cowboy-like, I was sittin' at the counter with my hat on. Cowboys never considered it impolite to sit at the counter with their hat on, but if they sit down at one of them tables they are supposed to take their hat off.

There was a bunch of town ranchers sittin' at a table behind me and they had been out to Dr. Harris's ranch and bought some registered cattle that day. I wasn't exactly eavesdropping but it was easy to follow by their conversation that they were going to ship these cattle to Sweetwater to a ranch that one of them had just bought. I could tell by the conversation that some oil wells had bought the ranch and that this town rancher didn't know too much about what he was doing and the men were worried about shipping the registered cattle in stockcars without a caretaker with them.

When I had finished my steak, I turned around to get up off my stool and I mentioned to them that I couldn't help overhearin' their conversation and wondered how many registered cattle they were shippin' in this stockcar. Well, Mr. Oilman Rancher spoke up and said they had eight bulls and four cows, and of course, he could tell quick by looking at me I would very well come in the category of caretaker and he quickly asked me if I wanted the job of riding in the stockcar to Sweetwater, Texas, with these cattle. Of course, the first dang thing that I asked him was how much he was goin' to pay and when was he goin' to load out.

This was Thursday and they were going to load out Saturday, and he would pay $50 for a good man to ride with them. He went on to tell me what all kinds of care he wanted them to have, and I told him that I would sure take the job with one understanding. I explained that a stockcar would carry about twenty-five cattle like he was talking about and there would be plenty of room left in the car to load three horses to take with me; I would unload them at Sweetwater after we had unloaded the cattle. Him and his "yes" men discussed this a little and didn't see that there would be anything wrong with it because he was having to pay a minimum charge for the car anyway and it wouldn't cost anything extra for my three horses.

We worked out the details and I got on the bus that night and went to Weatherford to get my horses and make my arrangements to be gone awhile and rode the horses back to Aledo, where the bulls were to be loaded, which was only about a fifteen-mile ride.

Everything went off fine. I took good care of their cattle on the trip and took good care of my horses by feedin' 'em some of the bulls' feed, unloaded them at Sweetwater, turned the cattle over to the man there that had been waitin' for them, and saddled up and started towards Snyder with my horses about Monday morning.

I camped at Hermleigh the first night. Next morning I rode through Snyder and turned west and camped on Bull Creek the next night. Then I turned north up Bull Creek about fifteen miles and found the pasture where my eight head of steers were supposed to be.

I rode the pasture out and it wasn't too big, maybe two thousand acres, but it was covered with real dense mesquite thicket with few open glades or high ridges in the pasture. I found the windmill, which was the only water in the pasture, and about a hundred yards from the windmill was a good set of corrals that had been built out of mesquite poles stuck in the ground maybe a foot deep with a cable running around the bottom of them about a foot from the ground and a cable running around the top about a foot from the top of the poles with a heavy post set about every ten feet with a cable tied to each big post. There was one big corral and two small ones fenced off of the west end of the big corral. And there was a water trough piped from the windmill built about in the middle of the big corral, and the fence that divided the two small corrals divided the water trough, so there would be water in all three corrals from one trough.

I had left my extra horses in one of the small corrals

while I rode out the pasture and got acquainted with it. When you start to make a camp in the pasture where you are tryin' to trap wild cattle, you need to make your camp out away from the water and the corrals where you are going to try to pen your cattle and where the prevailing winds won't carry your scent too bad. Since it seemed that most of the prevailing winds in that country would be from the south-southeast, I decided to go over to the west fence line about a quarter mile from the windmill on a high knoll where there were a few live-oak trees and make camp and wait till morning to start my hunt for my sight-unseen steer buy.

This was a real good location for a cowboy's camp. The knoll was just high enough up to be a little above the mesquite flats and would be in the evening shadows of the caprock and could enjoy a little more shade in the late afternoon because the sun would drop behind the caprock. Range cattle and old cowboys know that the breeze follows the draw and the foothills and the best night breeze would be up out of the draw and along the foot of the caprock, instead of high on the hill or deep in the valley like so many city folks would think about wind.

I had gotten pretty well acquainted with the fence line and how the pasture lay and knew that the windmill was toward the southwest corner and the worst of the thicket was up to the north and northeast. I felt pretty good about the fact that there was only one waterin' place in the pasture. I really didn't see why I just couldn't have waited for these cattle to come in to water and then, mounted on a sure-enough cow horse, headed and herded them until I could work them into that big corral gate, but this seemed a little too easy.

Next morning I saddled up early while it was still cool and decided to ride into the dense part of that mesquite thicket on the north end of the pasture and hunt for cattle. It didn't take more than an hour of poppin' the brush until I rode into these steers in the thickest part of the mesquite thicket, and they, in fact, were just gettin' up off their bed ground from the night before.

There were six bedded in a fairly close bunch and then there were two settled further up in the thicket away from these first ones. As I rode in, these cattle got up and stretched like any cow brute will do when it gets off the bed ground and, sure enough, they were great big steers strictly of Mexican origin, dark brindle-brown and solid-black colors with long, keen, well-set horns that showed they definitely had some Spanish fighting blood in their veins.

I whistled and hummed and rode through the thicket usin' both hands to get the limbs out of my eyes and rein my horse as carefully as I could, and I got pretty close before the steers decided to move off away from me, and I thought to myself, *These cattle are nearly gentle.*

I had the idea that I would push these cattle north against the fence line and hold them against the fence and drift them around to the west side about where I had made camp. This would throw them out onto a small prairie glade where I would try my luck at drivin' them in to water and into the big corral gate.

I rode along pretty quiet and didn't push these cattle too fast. When they came to the north fence line, of course, it was in dense, thick mesquite thicket, but I winged them to the west with no trouble and held my horse back away from them as they drove like common range cattle. We got around to the prairie glade that sloped in toward the windmill. My horse had broke into a good sweat and so had I, but it was just because the sun was up and the July day was gettin' hot. It wasn't from any extra runnin' we had done tryin' to work these steers.

There was a big water storage tank at the windmill that was built out of native rock, and the walls were about a foot thick and over six feet high and it was about ten feet across the tank. On the south side of this tank there was a drinkin' trough built with a common stock float in it to keep it from overflowing. It was about two feet wide and eighteen inches deep and built in the same circular formation as the storage tank, only it was just the length of the south side of the storage tank. This drinkin' trough was on the side of the storage tank facing the corral.

These eight steers were so big, horns and all, that they could just barely all get to the water trough at the same time. They stood there and drank and raised their heads and looked around. They were docile as any bunch of common cattle could be. When they had all finished drinkin', they all walked out to the open, facing me and my horse. I just made a little wavin' motion with my hand and slapped my leg like any cowboy would do when he wanted cattle to go the other way. When I did this, they raised their heads up, wrung their tails, and spread out fast, and I made a little circle like I was going to herd them back together, and as I passed each steer, it turned out behind my horse and headed for the thicket. It was the best original play that you ever saw pulled and there ain't no football team that had the precision work that those eight head of steers had. In less time than it took to stir the dust, I was standin' between the windmill and big corral gate on horseback and not a steer in sight. They had made it to the brush and was probably holdin' a little "bull session" for their own entertainment.

Any time a bunch of cattle get back to the thicket on you in the heat of the day, you just as well camp and make coffee 'cause you are not going to get much of a chance at them again that same day until the cool of the afternoon. I watered my horse and I was carrying water to my camp and had left a bucket down there that morning so I dipped my bucket of water and rode back to my camp, unsaddled my horse in the shade of a live-oak tree, and started cookin' me a batch of something for dinner. I had a batch of grub and took a nap. I didn't sleep too long because it was awfully hot. I raised up and gazed across the thicket where I thought those steers were shadin' and could see heat waves risin' up from the draw. I knew I needed to save myself and my horse so I managed to be contented to stay in camp until late afternoon.

I rode into these cattle and this time they weren't so gentle. They bawled a time or two and boogered and hit the thicket and you could hear brush poppin' a mile away. I rode till dark and never saw a steer.

I got out early the next morning and we had that same little morning exercise of goin' 'round the fence and into the water. After they had drank and started to make their play, I didn't try to head them. When the first one came by me, I took after him with a long rope and a big loop. When I set that rope around his horns, we were goin' about as fast as a steer can run. When my horse, Bob, set his feet in the ground to stop the steer, you could see that steer set his head and shoulders, and instead of hittin' the end of that rope limber, like any wild cow would do, he had set his head down at an angle that a work steer would set if he were on a hard pull, and when he hit the end of that rope and took the slack out, he popped it into right at the hondo where the rope fitted around his horns and the end of it flew back and stung me across the nose and the cheeks. Bob was taken by such surprise that he ran backward four or five steps before he got himself braced to keep from falling back. I heard the other cattle in the thicket bawlin' to the steer that I had caught and he answered in a tone of voice that sounded like he was tellin' 'em everything was all right.

I worked a full week at these cattle without making the slightest impression on them or without breakin' the even tenor of their ways of comin' in to water every morning between ten and eleven o'clock. I had set all the common-known snares made out of rope and concealed them with mesquite limbs across the trails in the pasture, which must have been a source of amusement to this bunch of steers since they had very carefully horned each snare so well out into the brush and out of the way of their leisure passage. Then I had begun to wonder what kind of a play it was goin' to take for me to begin to be a winner.

It was just a little before daylight when I was layin' on my pallet with this first week's failures runnin' through my mind when all of a sudden I had a real bright idea. I slipped out of bed and put on my clothes and saddled my horse that I had left tied to a tree that night and rode to the windmill. These cattle were so rank and on the prod that I didn't dare walk around in the pasture afoot. Even though I was going just a few hundred yards to the windmill, I had saddled my horse and went horseback.

I took my ax on the saddle with me, rode into the corral, and cut down a small mesquite tree about four inches around, then I cut about three feet off the trunk part of the tree, took me some wire, and ran this chunk of mesquite across the top of the water trough and tied the float up tight and with enough pressure against the mesquite to hold it in place. This way I was shuttin' off the water in the water trough at the storage tank. I took an old lard bucket and dipped the trough as nearly empty as I could get it, and my plan was that these cattle would would come in to water and stand around and paw and bawl a little while and even a day or so and would have to go into the big corral and drink out of the trough, which would give me a chance to hide and run out and shut the gate on some of 'em. This sure was a foolproof bright idea and I didn't know why I hadn't thought of it before.

Sure enough, way up in the morning they followed their usual trail out of the mesquite and across the glade and around the tank to the water trough. I stepped on my horse and went into the brush to work my way down the slope and around to the east side of the glade and waited for these steers to go into the big corral. I didn't much think they would the first morning, but, just in case, I wanted to be on hand to try my luck at gettin' the gate closed on some or all of 'em.

They smelled that dry trough and looked around the big storage tank. They hooked and played at one another a little since they weren't too dry, and I thought to myself that the next day they would want water enough to go into that corral, so maybe I had better not crowd them. After all, every time I crowded these steers they had either challenged me for a bullfight or else they had scattered and gone to the brush, and this wild cow hunt was just the reverse from most of them in that the damn cattle had got me afraid of them instead of makin' them afraid of me. They must have killed an hour or two before they drifted back into the mesquite to shade up before the heat of the day. I thought I ought to be as smart as a steer, so I shaded up too.

Since these cattle hadn't had a drink at their usual time, they made it back late that afternoon and I stood around horseback in the brush, but they never did go into the big corral. Along about night they drifted back out into the mesquite and I could tell that this little waitin' game we were playing was goin' to get monotonous for me. However, for the lack of a better plan and figurin' that the drier they got the easier they would be to put through that gate, I went back to camp and went to sleep feeling rather smart that up to now I was gettin' ahead of them.

I waited all the next morning and no cattle came in to water and this got me bothered because I knew unless they broke out of the pasture there was no other way for them to get water. I thought I had better ride out and see what had happened to them. So I saddled up in the middle of the afternoon after I had eaten my dinner, and on my way out I rode by the corral. Those eight steers had made a plain trail in the dry dust goin' through the gate into the big corral and had watered in the night and were feelin' no pain. I began to wonder when I would ever have more sense than a steer, so I got down and fastened that big swinging gate with the chain that was on it and then took some balin' wire and then wrapped around and tied it some more to be sure that these cattle didn't get in there that night.

I heard them walkin' and bawlin' in the night and rattlin' the gate with their horns, but when I got out there in the early morn, there was no sign of any steers. The weather being as hot as it was, I knew these cattle would have to water at least once a day and I felt like they would come in the next night and I would have the gate open and by some means I would figure out how to shut it fast after they went in.

I loafed around camp that day. A little after dark I still didn't dare go afoot, so I rode down to the corral and put my saddle horse in one of the small corrals with my saddle on, then I opened the gate and took a long rope and tied it to the gate and ran it along the ground back to the small corral. I figured that the partition fences were plenty good protection against these bad cattle, and I would have to get on my horse to do whatever I thought I was going to do to them after I shut the gate. I ran the rope through the fence to the same small corral where I had my horse. I laid down close against this pole fence, as much out of sight as I could possibly be, and waited for the big steers.

I dozed a little now and then and about midnight a noise woke me and I knew I about had my cattle caught. They milled around the trough where I had the water cut off and bawled and hooked one another and finally the big chocolate-colored steer came down and stuck his head through the gate and stood there. The one steer that usually ran with him came down and stood behind him and things were awfully quiet and still. I said to myself, "I'm goin' to get some of 'em if not all of 'em."

They smelled the ground and looked up and down the fence, and even though they hadn't found me, they were bound to have scented me and knew I was there. The other cattle moved down a little closer behind these first two, and some way or another in hooking at one another one of them stepped over the rope that was running on the ground across the gate; the feel of that rope was something strange, and when he boogered he stampeded the whole bunch and they went back to the thicket without water. That ruined the night's work.

I still thought this was a pretty good plan, so the next day I dug a little ditch and buried my rope and smoothed the dirt back over it with a limb to where it would look natural and took my stand that night, feelin' like maybe I was goin' to get some thirsty cattle to go into that big corral for water.

It was a hot, almost-still night with just a few top

leaves flutterin' in a breeze that was high above the ground. There was only part of a moon at this particular time, and my vision was not too good in the dark. Cattle can see a little way in the dark and their smell is extremely sensitive. About midnight or a little after, I heard the steers come in to water.

Many times wild cattle make less to no noise walking on a well-beaten-out trail; but because they are cloven-hoofed their toes will rattle as they pick up their feet. When you have trapped for wild cattle, you learn to listen and know what this sound means.

The night the steers boogered they didn't see me and I didn't think that they had quite figured out where I was, so I didn't move my hidin' place where I intended to lay until the cattle came through the gate and I could pull my rope to pull the gate closed. They first came to the dry water trough at the storage tank and stood around there bawlin'. Of course, they could smell the water in the water trough in the corral and they would walk back and forth between the corral fence and the storage tank, but it seemed that none of them were interested in takin' any chance on walkin' down the fence a few steps to try that open gate that would be an easy way in to water. I watched through a crack in the pole fence. It seemed to me like for half the night, but I am sure it wasn't for more than an hour or so. Every now and then a steer would lick or smell the bottom of that dry water trough and accidentally hit that tin float with a horn but this noise must have been familiar to them and it didn't cause any disturbance, but pretty soon I heard a worse noise and knew that it wasn't caused by just hittin' the tin float. Some big steer had hung both horns under the mesquite limb that I had tied the float up to with baling wire. This was a smart bunch of cattle about not being caught, but I didn't think that steer was smart enough to know what he was doing. I think that catchin' both horns was an accident, and it was causin' a certain amount of fright. When this big steer thought his horns were hung on something, he made a powerful lunge with his head and broke the baling wire and threw the mesquite limb over his back, and I heard the check valve in the float spewin' clear fresh water for a bunch of thirsty steers.

I raised up and saw them all scramblin' tryin' to drink at the same time and I thought that this might be my chance. I opened the gate and stepped on my horse and rode out into the opening and started hollerin' and hazin' these cattle, thinkin' I might crowd some of them into the big corral while they were still wantin' to turn back to that fresh water that they had only gotten a sip of. I was ridin' a big stout chestnut horse called Bob that had lots of cow savvy and was fast on his feet. When I rode into the cattle and squalled at them, it seemed to kill their thirst. Instead of showin' any interest in the water, they began to try to get away.

A horse has a reflector built into his eye that enables him to see better at night than cattle or men, and Bob was sure doing his part at trying to head them and hold them against that corral fence in an effort to push them in through the gate. In the flash of a second one of the big older steers came out of the black wad of cattle and charged me and Bob. Bob first set in to hold him and then saw that he was to be gored if he did and dodged as fast as he could and one horn opened the skin on the left shoulder on the point back to the cinch and ripped my britches leg open as he went by headin' for the thicket. The other cattle had taken the signal and were already out of sight. These old wild steers valued freedom more than water and just a short dry spell of two or three days hadn't caused them to think in terms of domesticity.

The next day I got up with the intentions of havin' me at least one steer roped, tied, run to death, or in a corral before night. After all, this was eleven days in a pasture without catchin' a single cow brute and if it was to get out it would damage my reputation as a wild cow hunter.

I started early and I boogered these steers in the brush, and I thought I would play it different. I turned them away from the water, rode and hazed and hollered and pushed them all morning. I didn't stop for dinner but about two thirty or three o'clock in the afternoon these cattle had scattered so bad that they had laid down and hid themselves in dense thicket and tall grass to where I couldn't even see a steer to holler at much less rope.

I was ridin' a tired horse from the south fence lines toward the corral and the windmill. We had both been wringin' wet with sweat several times, and the combination of dirt and salt caused from sweatin' had dried all over the back and arms of my shirt and in the hot sun it had begun to itch. I rode up to the water trough at the storage tank and as my horse drank and I drank a little from the trough, I just raised up and pulled off my shirt and was going to rinse the sweat and dirt out of it and put it back on wet. A shirt sure is cool in the heat of summer after you have rinsed it in a water trough.

This big storage tank made a little shade at this time of day on the north side of it. My horse snorted and took a few quick steps back away from the water trough on one side of me and I looked on the other side and there was this big chocolate-colored steer there. He had been shaded up on the other side of the water tank when I rode up and that was where he had gone when the bunch scattered.

He snuffed his nose and charged me fast and my only hope was to reach the windmill tower. As I turned to jump about two steps and get hold of the wooden cross braces on the windmill tower, he caught my left leg with one horn just along the shin and almost gave me what amounted to a foot lift as I grabbed the cross brace of the windmill tower and pulled myself barely out of his reach. He bawled and shook his head and jumped in an effort to reach me. Well, I had one boot heel hung over a crosspiece and clingin' with one hand and arm to the other crosspiece and fightin' at that steer with my shirt with the other hand. If a steer was about to get you cornered, it wouldn't make any difference what you had in your hand, even if it wasn't anything but a feather, you'd wave it at him.

Of course, I was squallin' at him at the top of my voice, but it didn't seem to put much fear in him. This everyday shirt was heavy cotton and drippin' wet. About the second or third lick I made at him, one wet sleeve wrapped around his horn, and I guess he thought that he had a piece of me because he made a kind of low, laughin'-like bawl and tossed his head so violently that he jerked the whole shirt out of my hand and the lashlike motion wrapped the other sleeve around the other horn. All of a sudden he stood still and I realized that steer looked better in a shirt than anybody that I had ever seen wearin' one because he was blindfolded completely and that wet shirt was stickin' close to his head.

I got a heap braver and the tone of my voice was a heap stronger, and when I bellered back at him he took a few steps backward. I eased to the ground as quiet as I could and went about one fourth of the way to the corral gate afoot. I whistled and hollered in not too unfriendly a tone and he turned and faced my direction but didn't make any move towards comin' at me. I took a little more chance and came a little closer and took some small rocks and hit him on the end of his nose, and when I did this he charged in my direction.

About that time a summer whirlwind passed me goin' toward him and I don't know what whirlwinds know about handlin' cattle but that steer came on full drive. I ran through the corral gate with him and closed it behind me and turned and slammed the gate and fastened it. The other steer had run off about one half mile and turned and watched the show and he bawled a time or two, just a lowlike call, and my blindfolded friend as yet hadn't offered to answer him.

By this time there was enough blood runnin' from the gash that the steer had made in the calf of my leg that it was sloshin' in my boot when I walked. My horse durin' all of this had gone over by the corral fence and was standin' easy, and I had no reason to try to catch him because he wouldn't leave me now.

There were some rocks built into the side of the storage tank that stuck out enough for a foothold, so that a man could climb up the side of the rock wall to see about the water in the big tank. And so I climbed up this rock, set up on the edge of the tank, and pulled my boot off my left foot. The windmill was runnin' just a little and there was a small stream of water runnin' out of the pipe into the tank, which was about the only clean water, so I sat there on the edge of the tank and let the cold well water run over the gash in my leg until it began to get cold enough to quit bleedin' and while I sat up there without my shirt on, I got a mild sunburn to add to my discomfort.

It had all happened pretty fast up until the time I crawled on the side of the water tank. I sat there and rested up some and rinsed the blood out of my boot and rinsed my sock and wrung it out while I was waitin' for that cold water to stop my leg from bleedin'.

By now, it was gettin' to be late afternoon so I crawled down carrying my boot and sock and crow-hoppin' over to my horse and rode up to camp feelin' like I had had a pretty good day. I had one steer in the corral a-wearin' a good shirt and a slight gash about three inches long in my left leg that I didn't consider to be serious. I washed ole Bob's shoulder off with soap and water and greased it with a salty bacon rind and unsaddled ole Beauty and fed the both of them. Peanut, my other horse, was runnin' loose in the pasture because I hadn't been usin' him.

While I had my boot off and my britches leg rolled up, I decided I had better do something to protect that open gash in my leg. A cowboy when he's out in camp rarely ever has any kind of medicine with him. If he bothered to think about how dangerous some of the things were that he did and make preparation to take medicines with him, he never would hunt bad cattle to start with.

I had used sugar to pour on open sores on horses sometimes, so I got my little cookin' outfit and poured this gash full of sugar. It would dissolve and form a hard scab and a little syrup would form under the scab and protect the sore from gettin' dirt and stuff in it.

I had a big supper of meat, beans, and taters and didn't have much trouble dozin' off to sleep. Up in the night about the time I had begun to get kinda rested, I woke up with that old leg givin' me a fit and when I got around and chunked up the fire a little to where I could see what the trouble was—sleepin' on the ground, the ants had moved in and was a-feastin' on that sugar scab. I had to sleep on the ground so I decided I had better wash that sugar scab off my leg. This took a little doin' to loosen and soften it up to pick the scabby pieces that had the sugar in them out of the deep part of the gash. I thought then that what I had done for Bob was probably what I should have done for myself, so I greased around it with that salty meat rind and managed to get back to sleep after a while.

I woke up about daylight and crawled off my pallet over against a big tree and propped up and watched the sun come up. My leg by this time was real sore and throbbin' pretty bad. Every once in a while that big brown-colored steer in the corral would let out a lonesome bawl and his runnin' mate would answer him up the draw a piece in the thicket. When the sun got up to where I could see good, I could tell that my leg was gettin' in pretty bad shape. There were big red streaks runnin' away from the gash and the edges of the gash had begun to open up and curl back and when I started to bend my knee, the hide was gettin' tight over my knee from the swellin' and I knew I had to do something for my leg before I tormented them big steers any more.

I wore long straight shank-spoke rowel spurs. The spokes were long but blunt at the ends and wouldn't cut a horse and it seemed that that was about the only thing in the way of a piece of iron that I had in camp that would do to sear out that sore. So I took the spur leathers off one spur and pushed the shank part into the coals of my campfire. I was a pretty tough young cowboy but I was beginnin' to wonder if there wasn't a limit to how tough I was when I got to thinkin' about that red-hot spur. I had a pair of horse-hoof nippers with me that I used to take that spur out of the fire and I took a good tight hold on it and drawed that leg up to where I could see what I was doin' and just set me a trail down through that sore with the rowel and shank of that spur. When I got through bitin' my lip and beatin' the ground with my fist and began to get my breath and tears quit runnin' out of my eyes, it sort of quit burnin'.

I laid around camp and pampered myself till after I had a batch of dinner, and you would be surprised how the red had faded out of that leg, and it just looked like I had a bad burn. It wasn't real sore as it had been that mornin' when I waked up. I got my sock and boot back on my foot and stuffed a little piece of scrap sheepskin in my boot top below the gash, which held my boot top out away from my leg, and I began to walk around and study about what I was going to do with my one big steer in the corral.

I rode down to the corral and opened the gate from horseback and started in, which was a big mistake. By this time the shirt had dried and was layin' over by the fence where the steer had rubbed it off. I didn't much more than crack the gate open when that steer started comin' at me and I backed my horse up real fast and slammed the gate. This gave me another bright idea. It wasn't goin' to be any trouble to rope over the fence because you could just ride up to the outside of the fence and shake it and he would charge and hit the fence.

I rode around to the back side of the corral and booed and boogered at him and caught his attention and here he came. When he was real close to the fence I pitched a rope over him and caught him around those great big long horns. I threaded the rope through a crack right next to one of the big heavy posts that were set deep in the ground that the rest of the fence was tied to and stepped off my horse in order to take the rope down low on the post before I took up the slack to tie the steer. I would just stick my hand through the fence and wave at him, and when he would charge the fence I would pull my hand back real fast and take up some more slack. I had him drawn to where he could touch the post by stickin' his nose out and the pole of his head between his horns was maybe eighteen inches from the post. I managed my rope back through the fence and took two extra wraps around his horns and back around the post to where he would have much less chance of breakin' the rope.

In handlin' real fightin' cattle, you learn to get their heads sore as soon as you can, then if you have to pull on them to do anything with them, they will give to that rope around their head without you putting forth too much force. I thought now that since I had him tied good and snug that I might open the gate and prop it back to see if his runnin' mate that had been standin' around just inside the thicket bawlin' and answerin' would show up.

It was gettin' late in the afternoon and this had taken longer than I thought it would, which didn't matter 'cause I wasn't goin' anywhere anyhow, so I rode off out to the pasture and thought I would give the rest of the cattle that I had chased so much a chance to water. Just about sundown, the same bunch (six head) eased out into the open and looked around awhile before they came up to water. The lone steer followed them and along about dusk the cattle drifted back out into the pasture except this lone steer that had been chummin' with the one I had tied in the big corral, and he went into the gate.

I was sittin' on my horse hid back in the brush about a quarter of a mile from the gate, but I had to cross the glade from the brush to the corral. The big water storage tank was between me and the gate so I rode out of the brush straight toward the big water tank hopin' the steer that was loose in the corral wouldn't see me until I got an even break to come from behind the water tank and beat him to the gate when he did discover me. This worked just right, and I had the gate slammed before he knew I was around. Now I had two steers. It was almost dark so I fastened the gate and rode back to my camp well satisfied with my day's work.

I was takin' time about ridin' Bob and Beauty, and since they were both gentle and would come to call, I would let one run out with Peanut at night, and I would keep one up in case I would have to have a horse in the night. Since all cowboys have the horror of being afoot, this is a habit they have that lay out in camp by their-selves. So I called my horses and fed them and had some supper and sat around camp and bathed my leg until the night began to get cool enough to go to sleep.

I was up early the next morning. I needed to rope this last steer and draw him up to one of the big heavy solid posts in the fence line and tie him close up to the post and let him work at gettin' his head sore the same as I had the other steer doin'. After this first steer I kinda had my system figured out about ropin' these steers from over the fence and drawin' them up without too much work on me or my horse and with a minimum amount of danger of gettin' horned. This was a lighter-colored steer and smaller than the first one, but in spite of his lack of size he had as much length of horn and they were just as sharp as the first one's. It stood to reason that the more cattle tied in that corral the better the chances were that the other cattle might come visitin', but since I had been giving them so much trouble, they seldom came to water until late in the afternoon.

As I looked at these steers' horns sticking through the fence, I thought how much better it would be for me and my horses—after all, I had one leg gashed and one horse's shoulder opened by horns—if these horns were tipped back about two or three inches to where they would be blunt in case I had any more trouble with them. And, it would be a good idea if I could tip the horns when I caught 'em. (I didn't let myself think, '*If* I caught them.')

I hadn't been to anybody's town since I set up camp and had begun to run a little short of grub. I thought that Fluvanna would be about the closest place to where I was camped so I took a general direction, let down a few fences and tied them back on the way until sure enough, I came upon a ridge about middle of the morning, and Fluvanna was on the other side of the draw. I had struck a dim road and I saw that it led on down to a wire gate that opened out into the public road, and it was only a couple of miles further on over to the town of Fluvanna.

This town wasn't too hustlin' and bustlin', but there was a good mercantile, Fluvanna Mercantile Company, and some other stores. I tied my horse to a mesquite tree across the road west from the mercantile and decided to take in the whole town.

I started in by eatin' some cookies and a can of peaches and the other kinds of sweet stuff that a cowboy don't get campin' out, and visitin' with the storekeeper. He was kinda polite but he sorta figured it part of his business to find out who I was and what I was doing and didn't consider it a matter of buttin' in. When I told him where I was camped and about the cattle, he held a rather poker-like face and didn't show any particular interest in what I had told him.

I bought a small batch of grub about what I could put in a toe sack and tie on the back of my saddle. I knew he wouldn't have a dehorning saw so I asked to buy just a regular carpenter's hand saw. He said, "You got a hammer and some nails?" and I answered, "No, but I'm not goin' to need any."

He said, "Well, I thought you might from what I hear'd about them steers. I supposed you might be aimin' to build you a house to winter in."

I said, "Don't let that bother you none." As long as I had trapped and fought bad cattle, I didn't aim to let no remarks of a mild-mannered, quiet-livin' country storekeeper unnerve me, so for a quick answer I said, "I'm goin' to saw every one of that bunch of steers feet off to the quick and they'll be so tender that they drive easy."

This kinda set him back because I could tell by lookin' at him that he couldn't tell how I was going to saw their feet off if I couldn't catch them. Of course, I was lyin' a little, but it was a ready answer, and I didn't have to give my plans away. In that it would matter only when cowboys are trying a fresh trick on something; if it didn't work you didn't have to face any music for any previous notice you had put out.

He told me a little better way to get back to the pasture than the one I had come by and I rode into camp a little before dark, and I guess the wild cattle had already watered judgin' by the signs around the water trough.

The next morning I knew that I was going to have to water these steers that I had tied up so I took a water bucket and tied a rope on the bucket handle and dipped some water and let it down over the fence to the first steer. He smelled of it and bawled and hooked it right back in my face. I said to myself that if he wasn't thirsty enough to improve his manners any more than that, I

wouldn't bother about him for another day or two; I
didn't offer the other one a drink at all.

Just in case these two steers might by some foul
means get loose, I thought I just as well saw the tip ends
of their horns off this morning. They had their heads up
close to the post and their horns naturally stuck through
the fence and I figured I could push against a horn hard
enough to hold the steer with one hand and use the saw
with the other hand. I was countin' on cuttin' these keen
points back to where the blunt ends of the horn would be
about an inch across where I sawed it off. That part of a
steer's horn is solid with no feeling in it but would keep
him from being able to do much damage, like maybe
opening my other leg.

I got hold of a horn and started sawing, and I guess
the vibrations and sound wasn't too soothin' to that old
outlaw steer. He began to bawl and fight the post and
push his horn around through the fence and offer considerable objection to whatever he thought I had in mind.
The morning was hot and still and me and that steer both
got plenty well worked up, and I just had the tip of one
horn sawed off about like I thought it ought to be. I quit
and went to camp and shaded up till late afternoon
thinkin' that a little more time and a little sorer head
would make that steer dehornin' a little less troublesome.

Along late in the afternoon I greased my saw with
some lard thinkin' it might make it cut better and stepped
on Beauty and rode back down to the corrals. Now a cow
brute's horns are shaped and set at the base of the head
into the skull to where it's next to impossible to break a
horn from a straight lick or where the pressure would

push between the horn spread from point to point backward against the skull. The most common way that a horn gets broken off at the skull is by a hard lick from the outside of the horn driving into the center of the horn spread. Pressure or a sudden lick can loosen or knock a horn off real quick. I started to saw on the other horn on this old big brown-colored steer and in his scuffin' and fightin' somehow he managed to get his right horn on the left hand side of that big post and threw the pressure against it from the outside and when he hit it with all his weight he knocked his own horn off at the base of the skull, leaving enough stub to hold the rope. He was mad and hot and a fine spray of blood squirted clear to the top of that fence and on the ground for about five or six foot. Not more than a few minutes later I heard an awful lot of bawlin' comin' from the thicket up the draw.

People that don't know might not realize how much difference there is in the tone and expression of the bawl of a cow brute. Old-time cowmen can tell from a distant bawl whether it's a cow, steer, or a bull by the tone and the long or short of the sound. Other things that can be told by the tone of a bawl is whether a cow has lost her calf and is bawling for it to answer her, or if it's a stray that's lost from the herd. Sometimes cattle will make different tones of noises when they are bawling at the change of weather, and when cattle are excited by the presence of animals of prey, such as panthers or wolves, the tone of their call takes on a considerably higher pitch. There are other circumstances or conditions that can be determined from the tone and pitch of the noise that the cattle are making when they bawl. The most blood-curdling of all these different sounds is when primitive or cold-blooded cattle smell blood and they can actually tell the difference between cow blood and other kinds. I knew real quick that the faint afternoon breeze had carried the smell of blood to the rest of the wild steers the same as the whirlwind had carried the scent of blood from my leg when the steer followed me into the corral. They moved in a close bunch out of the thicket and into the opening with their heads high and continued their high tone of savage bawlin'.

This old steer had bled for about thirty or forty minutes real bad, and when it began to taper off the weather was so dry that the blood dried quickly on the ground and on the fence and I guess the scent faded out on the wind, but the steers up the draw didn't offer to go back into the brush. It was late enough in the afternoon for them to come to water, and they weren't making any move like they intended to come in. I just thought that maybe in the cool of the afternoon or just maybe at dark that a strong scent of blood on the early night wind might bring these old steers into the corral. Because of that gash in my leg, I felt like I had considerable score to settle with this old boy who had knocked his horn off, and I couldn't see how he would need just one horn for anything.

I rode back to camp and got me a clean empty lard bucket and my poleax. A poleax has a single blade and the back part of the ax is wide and flat and heavy, to be used for driving fence posts or poles, and I guess that's where they get the word poleax.

Just about dusk I had already opened the gate and

propped it back and tied a long rope on the bottom and at
the end of the gate so I could jerk it closed without having to stand in the gate opening. I wanted to make it easy
for these old steers to come in. I put another rope around
his neck and tied it so he would not choke and tied this
rope to the fence, in case the horn made a clean break
and the horn rope came off the neck rope would still have
him tied. Then I took my poleax and took dead aim and
with all my strength I hit that other horn at the same
angle as the bull had hit the one against the post and it
popped and flew off into the air. I grabbed my lard bucket
and followed that spray of blood around that was
squirtin' from that steer's head till I had blood all over me
and had about half a bucketful before he stopped
squirtin' blood to where I could catch it in the bucket,
and in the next few minutes the blood-curdling bawlin'
noises from the wild steers that had by now moved well
out into the glade sounded loud and clear.

I went by the water trough and washed the blood off
my hands and face and threw enough water on my
clothes to kill the scent and hurried and climbed up to
the top of the windmill tower and began to let a little
dribble of blood pour from the lard bucket. As the
bawlin' came closer I would spill out a little more blood
on the wind. By spilling a little blood from the top of the
windmill, the scent would carry farther than dried blood
squirted on the ground.

By now there was some moonlight and these cattle
were fightin' each other between short runs toward the
smell of the blood. When they did stop, I would dribble a
little more of that warm blood into the night air and here

they would come again. By the time they were close to
the windmill, I was high enough above them that they
couldn't get my scent and I guess, too, that the steer
blood would have overcome what human scent there
would have been on me. There was a little blood left in
the bottom of the bucket, but I quit pourin' any out and
sat breathlessly still waitin' for them to pick up the scent
of the bloody steer and the blood on the fence as being the
scent they were followin' instead of what I had been
pourin' out of the bucket.

They had gotten close enough now and I had been
gone from the corral long enough so that the cattle in the
corral began to answer, and whether any music teachers
believe it or not, there was a plaintive tone difference in
the bawlin' of the steers tied and the ones comin' in.

They passed the windmill and water trough without
stopping to drink and ran into the corral to where the two
steers were tied. They attacked the steer that had his
horns knocked off and blood all over him, from both sides
like they intended to destroy him and get him out of his
misery.

While this fightin' was going on I got down off the
windmill, pulled the gate shut, and wrapped my rope
around the gate and gatepost three times and tied it hard
and fast. The next thing I had to do was to untie that one
steer before they horned him to death. I hurried around
to the back side of the corral, and he was fightin' to get
loose and these steers were pitchin' him back and forth so
that big heavy post was actually wavin' in the air in spite
of how deep it was set in the ground. I took my knife and
cut the rope. It wouldn't have been possible to untie it

with all that pullin' and pressure that that old steer was puttin' on. As he came loose and went to runnin' around in an effort to get away from these other cattle, their beastly instinct seemed to have told them that he was free and they quit fightin' him.

I had eight big outlaw steers in a corral and my problems may have just started instead of being settled. I went back to camp and slept very little as these cattle walked and bawled and I could hear horns clashin' all through the night.

Every bright idea that I had durin' the night about gettin' my wild steers out to the public road was going to take more big rope than I had with me, and I thought it would be best when I started in on these cattle not to stop or allow them any rest. The way I figured it, I was going to need more rope to tie the steers to the fence and rope to yoke them together in pairs, so I thought I had better go back to Fluvanna to that mercantile and get some more rope before I started the war.

As I rode past the corrals, I noticed that this bunch of old wild cattle, either in fun or because they were trapped, had marked each other's hides up pretty bad in the night with their horns. This corral fence was a big stout fence and the uneven jagged points made by the poles at the top of the fence would cause them to be much less likely to try to jump out or try to push over than if it were a plank fence with cracks in it and a smooth plank around the top, so I didn't much think there was any danger of them trying the fence during the day that it would take me to go to Fluvanna and back.

I rode the horse Peanut into town a little before noon

and this old storekeeper couldn't help but show a little shock when I told him that I needed about two hundred feet of three-quarter- or one-inch rope to tie my big steers with. He pulled it off a long coil that was under the counter and marked it off by the tacks that were driven in the counter for the purpose of measuring rope. This was a right smart coil of rope, and I took it out and tied it on my saddle. Then I thought I would eat a bunch of can grub for dinner so I turned and went back to the store. The old man had one of them big community bowls under the counter that he wiped out with a piece of paper on his elbow for me to pour some can grub in for dinner.

We was visitin' all the time and I had noticed a little pair of fat bay horse mules over the fence from where my horse Peanut was tied, and among some of the other bright ideas that I had a pair of mules would help my plans. So I up and asked the old storekeeper, "Wonder where I could trade for a pair of little mules?"

He brightened up considerably and said that last year's schoolteacher had made a little failure at a crop and before the schoolteacher had moved that spring, he had swapped him a pair of little mules in on the grocery bill, and he would be easy to deal with if I could use them.

I already had my suspicions that these mules belonged to the store because this was a small trap pasture that they were in across the road from the store and there was kind of a mixed-up little bunch of cattle in the same pasture with them. I asked him how he would trade for a nice gentle saddle horse.

Peanut was a little small but that wasn't his worst

trouble. He was a horse that cowboys would refer to as not havin' any "heart." He was a little on the lazy side and couldn't stand to much ridin' and when you would tie rope or something on him, he couldn't stand pain and pull and I didn't mind tradin' him off.

Mr. Storekeeper said he had more use for a saddle horse than he did them mules and one would eat less than two and he would try to trade with me. I finished up my pork and beans, crackers, gingersnap cookies, and Coke, and we walked across the road to look at his little mules.

They were little fat mules and maybe weighted 800 pounds a piece, and you could tell at a glance that their mamas were bound to have had kinfolk in Mexico. It didn't take me long to swap my horse and $20 for this pair of little mules. They were eight to ten years old and had been worked and rode and were plumb gentle, so I put my riggin' on one and cut a short piece off that big coil of rope and tied it around the other mule's neck and started back to camp ridin' a mule and leadin' a mule.

It was late when I rode in. My cattle were all right and there was water in the corral. I took the bucket and watered the second steer that was still tied. His manners were improved and he was glad to drink four bucketsful as I carried it to him. The other cattle hadn't begun to show much shrink from lack of grazing yet.

That night I cut my rope into twenty-foot lengths and raveled the ends and tied good, hard knots and rolled the ends on a rock with my foot to be sure that they were gonna stay tight. This rolling breaks down the rope to where you can pull the knot tight and it won't come loose.

Next morning I saddled my standby, Beauty, and started in roping these steers over the fence and pulling them over to the big heavy posts that were about ten feet apart in the fence line and tying them hard. I took time out for me and my horse to eat dinner and went right straight back to work even though the summer sun was beatin' down pretty hot. By late afternoon I had tied every one of these big wild steers to a big gentle post and had sawed a little piece off the end of all seven steers' horns.

The next morning I started early and since all the steers were tied I could go into the corral and not be working over the fence, which made it a lot handier. I would pitch a rope over a steer's neck and give it a whip-like motion to where the knot would come back under his neck on the ground back on my side. These old cattle would wring their tails and bawl and kick at me but as long as I stayed against their neck and shoulders I stood a pretty good chance of not gettin' kicked. When I got the rope tied around one steer's neck, I pitched it over the next steer from him, and as I loosened the rope that he was tied to the post with, I would let it slip two or three feet and take up the slack on the loose rope around the other steer's neck until I got them pulled together. When I had them as close together as I could get them, I would tie around the steer's neck that I had been pullin' on with a bowline knot, then I would give the steer that I had left tied fast that I had pulled to slack so he could back away from the post and they could both stand with their heads up. I had to go in and out of the corral and give them slack from where I had tied them, and it took me just about all day to yoke these eight head of cattle to four pairs, and even though I had given them slack I still hadn't untied any of them from the fence.

That night I packed all my campin' gear together and had it ready to move out next morning. All I left out was a skillet and a few little things to cook with, and I could roll my bed up next morning.

I was up early, fixed my breakfast, and packed all my belongings on Bob. I had another saddle and another packsaddle that I rigged the two mules up with. Both the saddle and the packsaddle had big, heavy cinches front and back and breast collars. I led all of them to the corral and dropped the lead rope on Bob so he could graze until I was ready for him. He wouldn't run off with the pack.

I took one of the little mules into the corral and made sure that his riggin' was all good and tight. I flipped a rope around until I got it wrapped over the yoke rope across between one pair of steers. I managed to get up to the other side of the steer and get hold of the knot. I stepped back from the steer and made a slip knot and pulled it down tight on the yoke rope between the two steers.

These little mules didn't seem to have much fear so I led the first one in and tied that rope that I had just put on the yoke rope to the back ring of the cinch riggin' on the saddle. These old steers weren't liking all of this messin' around but still didn't seem to be dead set on killin' anybody that morning after they had been tied to that fence about a day and a night. I got a rope rigged up on another yoke of steers on the other side of my mule and tied to the back ring of the cinch riggin' on the other side. I knew that a little mule couldn't drag four steers far, and I also knew that the steers couldn't run backward and drag the mule very far and I didn't believe they could horn him runnin' forward because a mule in most every circumstance will wind up by takin' good care of himself. But before I rigged up the other mule, I decided I would turn these steers loose from the fence and see what the show was going to be like.

I untied the rope from the fence but I left all the head ropes on the steers and draggin' on the ground, thinkin' that while they stepped on the drag ropes and while they were learnin' to walk without stepping on them, it would give my mule a little better chance at survival. I got on Beauty and took a bull whip and started these steers and this mule on into the middle of the big corral. One or other of these big steers had taken a lick or two at the little mule and since their horns had been tipped back with the saw, they had made a little mark on the hide of the mule but hadn't cut into the flesh. This is the main reason that I had tipped these horns to start with.

The mule worked his ears and had turned his head around to keep an eye on his playmates. It wasn't easy for any one steer to run at the mule since they were yoked together, which gave him a lot of protection, but one pair had eased around close enough that the one steer raked him up the hind leg. By this time, Mr. Mule was gettin' smart so he proceeded to stand on his forelegs and kicked these steers in the face, head, and up and down the legs and shoulders about half a dozen licks before they realized that he had a mad on. I felt like that my plan was workin' right so I went through the same action of gettin' the other four steers tied to the other mule.

By mid-morning I turned two mules, eight steers, and my pack horse out on the trail that would lead to the public road west of Snyder where Bull Creek crossed the public road. The steers ran astraddle some mesquite sapling but the separate yoke pairs never did get badly mixed up with the other yoke that was being led·by the same mule. I had a ten-foot bull whip with a revolving handle in it that I used to my complete satisfaction any time the steers got unruly, but I never did have to hit the little mules. Of course, Bob followed along and watched the excitement and carried the pack and Beauty seemed to enjoy the whole episode since this was something different from the other few thousand things that she and I had done together.

In the beginning these steers would get to hurryin' one of those little mules and I had a few runaways, and there was one time when my two sets of oxen were a half a mile apart and they were still tied to a mule apiece, but with enough ridin' and enough bull whippin' I put them back together.

I went through two fair-sized pastures followin' a narrow road through the mesquite until I came out on a country road that led down to what was a public road, or maybe called the highway; however it wasn't a paved road and turned east toward Snyder.

It was gettin' late afternoon and I had begun to wonder what I was goin' to do with my pets for the night. After seven or eight miles out of Snyder I saw a small set of corrals settin' out in the pasture a little piece from the road, and a wire gate at the road that would let me into these corrals, so I knew that me and my pets had found bed ground for the night.

It was customary among stockmen of the Old West to use corrals or small water traps anywhere they found them. It was considered nice to ask somebody if there were people anywhere close to the corral but it wasn't thought to be bad manners when you were driftin' across the country to pen your stock anywhere you found a place; and whether you did or didn't see the owner, it was generally known that you were always welcome to use whatever you needed to hold your drive overnight. And, it's good to know and I take pride in saying that this is still the custom among stockmen of the West.

I rode around my steers and mules and opened the gate and dropped back and waited for them to come through. The little mules were doing a heroic job of leadin' and jerkin' the steers—just for instance, it would have been a fair job of cowboyin' to have put these steers through that gate, but the little mules were broke and gentle and lookin' for gates and led the steers right on through. The same was true when I set the gates and drove them into the corral where I was going to leave them for the night.

The big corral hadn't been used in a long time and was grown up in grass and weeds and the steers might not fill up but they could get some pickin' during the night. I stayed on my horse and eased up against the mule's shoulder and untied the steers' lead rope from the cinch rings, but I didn't unyoke the steers from one another.

I took the little mules into a small corral and unsaddled them and got my pack off Bob, which had some oats in it, and fed the mules and ole Beauty, but I was runnin' short of oats and Bob had loafed along and grazed all day so I just gave him a double handful to keep his feeling's from being hurt.

By that time it was good dark and I talked myself out of buildin' a fire and fixin' supper because I could see some glow in the east and knew that Snyder would have to be about seven or eight miles from where I was. Bob had had an easy day, so I turned Beauty loose and sad- dled Bob and rode into Snyder.

It was about eight thirty when I got to town, and of course I headed for a big batch of café cookin', and ate up everything I ordered and wiped the plate clean with the last piece of bread. I didn't try to take in the town picture show, but I rode about a block down on the north side of the square in the flat where I found some traders' pens, and I knew then I would pen my cattle and spend most of tomorrow around Snyder and do some restin' and loafin' and maybe sell some big steers. I rode back to camp and bedded down with my stock for the night.

It was about sunup when I put the riggin' back on the mules and led them to the big corral to tie the steers back to 'em. These bad cattle were drawn and sore and had lots of the fight taken out of them by the rough use they'd had for the last couple of days, and it wasn't any trouble to ease 'round and pick up the lead rope that I had left on each yoke of steers. I went about leadin' the mules a little and drivin' the steers a little until I got them all back about like they belonged, put my pack on Bob and rode Beauty and started to Snyder.

The grass was good in the ditch along the side of the

highway. The steers and the mules grazed a lot and didn't drive very fast and it was about noon before I made that seven or eight miles into Snyder. I turned north at the edge of the business part of town and followed Deep Creek around to the flat north of the courthouse square where I had spotted the traders' pens. I saw some fellers visitin' and a-whittlin' and shaded up next to a small barn about half a block away and hollered at them that I needed some place to pen these cattle. A feller, who I later learned was Bill Taylor, stepped down the fence a piece and held the gate open and hollered, "Bring 'em on."

After we had the gate closed and I went to untyin' the steers from the mules, the horse and cattle traders had begun to gather 'round and look at these big steers, and even then they were something to see. There was some comment from the boys with maybe a farmer background that they had never seen cattle led before by tyin' them to a mule. Of course, some of the others spoke up that was a good way to handle them. I put my mules and saddle horses away in another corral and got a bale of alfalfa hay for them and put my saddle and packsaddle way back under a feed trough next to a fence and me and this Bill Taylor went off uptown to eat some dinner.

He was a right friendly, helpful kind of a feller, and I explained to him how come I had these steers and I would like to sell them or figure out a way to get them to Weatherford. During our eatin' and visitin' he didn't come up with any ideas about gettin' them sold, and there weren't enough stock to afford a car on the Roscoe, Snyder, and Pacific Railroad that would later run into the

Texas and Pacific goin' to Weatherford. We were both of about the same opinion that these steers ought to be worth $50 or $60 a head.

Bill was mostly interested in horses and didn't care a whole lot about the steer business. He asked me if I knew where there were some flashy-colored-lookin' stylish saddle horses that could be bought worth the money. He said that Clint Sheppard had a contract to buy the horses to be used on the Texas Centennial Cavalcade and he had been through a few days before going west. He thought Clint would be back any time now and he wished that he had a horse or two that would fill the specifications because Clint was givin' a little premium for the kind that he wanted.

I told him that I thought I would spend the rest of the day and the night if he wasn't in need of the pens I was takin' up and he said, "Oh, no." He told me I could stay as long as I wanted to and let my stock rest and fill up and then they would travel better. I spent the rest of the afternoon loafin' around Stinson Brothers (Lee and Joe) Drugstore and bought me a new work shirt and pair of britches at Rogers Dry Goods Store on the west side of the square. That night I ate supper and went to the picture show and stayed in the Manhattan Hotel on the south side of the square.

Of course, cowboy-like, I waked up before daylight and decided I had better get out of that soft bed before I got spoiled and learned to like it and get back down to the tradin' pens, feed my saddle horses and mules, so I would be ready to drift my stock out of town early. These old mesquite-grass steers had sure took a likin' to that good alfalfa hay and fresh town water and had filled up and looked a whole batch better.

I got everything rigged up and tied together and turned out of the tradin' pens after it was good sunup and started down the road toward Roscoe, which was on the main line of the Texas and Pacific Railroad. I had hoped that I might find some cattle being shipped along the Texas and Pacific and somebody might have an odd half a car where I could make a trade to ship with them to Fort Worth.

These old sore-headed steers had learned to lead real good and had quit tryin' to fight. Up about mid-morning I began to wonder about untyin' 'em from the little mules and let everything just graze along together. I eased up beside the little mules and talked to them and got them to stop and untied the steers' lead ropes. These old steers had kinda learned to walk with each other since they had been tied together going on three days and nights and even thought they were draggin' a head rope apiece and a lead rope to step on every now and then, they were grazin' and walkin' and gettin' along pretty good and it seemed the little mules were enjoyin' considerable relief from havin' the cattle tied to them, and drivin' the herd had settled down to nothin' much more than grazin' and fol-lowin' along behind them since it was a real wide-like highway where the railroad and highway ran along to-gether and there were good fences on both sides.

It was a little after dinnertime when we drove through Hermleigh and I stopped at a store and got some cheeze and crackers and stuff that I could eat while I rode along and keep my stock grazin' and driftin' along down the road.

That night I penned my stock at Wastella Switch. This had been a pretty good day's drive for my steers and still at the same time hadn't moved them so fast but what they were full and would bed down and rest durin' the night. I made camp at the stock pens and nothin' good or bad happened, and I turned out early the next morning still driftin' south and east toward Roscoe.

I drove my stock around the back side of the stores at Roscoe and by the gin and out onto the Sweetwater highway east of town. Since I had kept them movin' pretty good, I thought that if I just left them along the road that they would stop and graze while I rode back about half a mile to Roscoe and eat a batch of stuff.

When I got back out to my stock, I found a car stopped, my steers grazin', and my mules standin' over by the side of Bob against the right-of-way fence line restin'. I didn't guess the car had been there very long and as I rode up, two well-dressed, past-middle-age-lookin' fellers went to gettin' out of the car and one of them said, "Do you belong to these steers?" and I said, "That's a pretty good way of puttin' it."

As the man got out of the other side of the car and turned around, I recognized it to be Clint Sheppard. I had known Clint and his father about all my life since they had both been very prominent in the mule and registered jack business, and I had been seein' Clint at the Fort Worth horse and mule market ever since I could remember.

As the conversation went, Clint was buyin' horses for the Texas Centennial, as I already knew from Bill Taylor, and this other feller was buyin' the cattle to be used in the Cavalcade. They had been out West huntin', from what this man described, "picturesque" steers. I didn't know whether that was a breed or a color but I aimed for these I had to be what he was lookin' for. He walked around and looked at these cattle and they were so jaded and had so many ropes on them that they didn't offer to try to get away from him or try to fight him, and it was plain to see that they were sure use to being handled, which was just what he needed in some big long-horned odd-colored steers. Of course, he had already begun to offer objections about the big brown steer that had both horns knocked off.

In the meantime, while he was lookin' at the cattle, Clint and I had been visitin', renewin' old acquaintance. Clint was a nice-lookin' feller and was always well dressed and well spoken, but he had one eye gotched off a little bit to the side. He was behind my horse from the fellow lookin' at the cattle, and from some mule deals in the past, he may have thought that he owed me a little favor, and compared to him I was just a kid.

When the other man asked what I wanted for *seven* head, Clint winked at me with that gotched eye and said, "Ben, I guess you'll have to sell them all together. You ain't got no business with one steer." I got the message pretty fast because sure enough, I didn't need one sore-headed steer.

Well, the trade started and the other man said he couldn't give as much for them a head if he had to take that one. I said, "Well, I will knock off a little. How would $90 round sound to you?"

Of course, I knew in my own mind that it was goin' to

sound damn high, but he didn't know how much I could afford to take off to sell them. He acted like he was about to lose his breath and he never heard of such a price and by this time, I kinda figured out what that word meant, and I said, "Yeah, but you ain't bought any 'picturesque' steers neither, have you?" Clint busted in real good and said, "No, we've been lookin' for them all this trip. There's no more cattle that are that big with as long horns and as flashy colors, and I can't imagine where Ben found these!"

We passed a lot more conversation among us, and this fellow finally said that $75 a head was all that he would give for my cattle and I could take it or leave it. Well, I didn't aim to leave it, so I said, "Where do you want me to put 'em? I'm goin' to sell 'em to you." That brought on some more talk and he decided that if I would put them in the stock pens at Sweetwater that he would pay me for them. I saw Clint smile and cut that white eye back at me as much as to say that I had made a good deal.

Sweetwater wasn't more than about seven miles, and I perked these cattle up and drove them on in to the stock pens at Sweetwater by about five o'clock and, sure enough, he gave me a check for $600. I didn't ask them whether they was goin' to ship them by rail or make baloney sausage because I sure didn't care; I was rid of them and had made money. The trip home with two saddle horses and two nice fat mules would be as enjoyable as a sightseein' tour.

WILD COWS IN
DRIPPIN'
SPRINGS SOCIETY

DRIPPIN' SPRINGS CANYON PASTURE
is a very famous landmark in the open prairie country
of West Texas. As far as the eye can see in every direct-
tion is a big rolling Texas prairie. The prairies have a
gentle slope to the south and east, and suddenly drop off
into a huge canyon that is not noticeable until you are
right to the brink of it. The canyon walls are steep but do
have enough slope to them that the walls are covered with

catclaw and live oak and small shinnery brush. At the bottom of the canyon there is a little narrow open floor that is dotted with beautiful live-oak trees. At the head of the canyon is a large hole of water fed by springs and is known as Clear Hole. All up and down the canyon for the length of it, which is about three miles, there are drippin' springs flowing out of the rock walls that give the landmark its name. This canyon and a small amount of prairie land around the rim makes up a pasture that is owned by the village banker that could be very easily referred as "Ole Spendthrift."

Drippin' Springs Canyon has been the setting for many festive occasions for the little town and the range country around it. There is a huge barbecue pit and a few tables and chairs in the live-oak grove where political speakin's, ole settlers' reunions, Sunday-school picnics, and all kinds of school outings have been held since the Palefaces took the land away from the Indians.

Ole Spendthrift had always let on that he was a very civic-minded citizen and that ever'body was welcome to enjoy the landscape and the facilities of Drippin' Springs Canyon. It had become the custom of the community, since there was no other beauty spot around, that everything of any social nature that happened outdoors happened in Drippin' Springs Canyon.

But here of late there had been a sad situation developing that none of the community was happy about, and Ole Spendthrift seemed to be a little disturbed. He had sold off all the cattle that could be rounded up out of Drippin' Springs Canyon. However, there had been a remnant of wild old cows that refused to leave their native haunts and had developed a hostile attitude toward the human race. These ole cows had gotten on the prod and were ready to take on any bunch of people that might think they wanted to picnic in the floor of Drippin' Springs Canyon. They had scattered a covey of Boy Scouts up the canyon wall without any of 'em gettin' seriously hurt. They tore up a Ladies' Aid party, but the ole women all manged to get to their cars. These wild ole cows had just about ruined the social affairs of the community for the entire summer. Even to ruinin' the Fourth of July political speakin'. None of this seemed to disturb Ole Spendthrift. It looked like he had decided that he'd ruther have that little bunch of ole outlaw cows than to have the good will of the community. And he'd made little or no effort to get these cows trapped or drove or by some means caught up out of the community's playground.

Miss Effie Comstock was a very petite, precise, and ultra-refined old maid . . . who came West when she was a very young woman to bring culture and musical appreciation to the range country. She had pretty well aged-out on the job, but had never given up and, to be sure, she had a great deal of influence on the younger set in the community. She had started her fall music school, and by the admission of their own mothers, her young ladies' music classes were filled with the finest flowers of young womanhood in the range country.

Us cowboys didn't hold Miss Effie in the same high regard as the rest of the community, and the reasons were very evident. She discouraged "her young ladies" from keepin' company with the uncouth element of the community and when she saw one of her "young ladies" in town in the company of a cowboy, she would give the cowboy about the same appraising look that a registered thoroughbred Kentucky mare would give if she suddenly saw a Spanish burro. And this failed to cause us to feel too kindly toward Miss Effie. We very respectfully referred to her as the "shrill and shriek teacher" or sometimes "Miss Cornstalk" or anything else that might come to our minds just so long as it was not profane or vulgar.

Miss Effie decided as a prelude to the fall music school that she and her "young ladies" this particular Sunday afternoon would take basket lunches and drive out to the live-oak grove in the bottom of Drippin' Springs Canyon and gaze upon the colors that nature's paintbrush had splashed over the countryside. She and the girls had spread their picnic lunch and were carrying on all the feminine niceties that they should show towards each other for the benefit of Miss Effie. Some of these wild old longhorn brindle cows that had not received proper invitation to the outing took direct offense to havin' been left out, and as they started to Clear Hole to get a drink of water decided to mix and mingle with these fair damsels.

Well the screech-and-scream class really went into action! These ole gals bawled about twice and made a head-on run for the crowd. If rodeo cowboys think they invented jumpin' in barrels, they are mistaken. Miss Effie rose and lit in the trash barrel, and all the flowers of young womanhood scooted up these live-oak trees faster than any school of squirrels could've ever thought of. One ole cow hit the barrel Miss Effie was in and jarred a stave loose, and that jarred some staves that Miss Effie had on! Miss Effie reached high "C" in such voice that it boogered the ole cow, and she took to the brush without gettin' a drink of water. Another longhorn ole cow grabbed that checked tablecloth and garnished the landscape with tuna-fish sandwiches, deviled eggs, and ladyfinger cookies.

This four or five head of cows had decided that they'd delivered a sufficient welcome and drifted on back up into the canyon.

So Miss Effie's "shriek and shrill" girls came down out of the trees and got Miss Effie out of the trash barrel and hastily departed, leaving little patches of bloomer material of various colors on the snags of that live-oak thicket, clear to the topmost limbs!

On Sunday night if a cowboy got a date with one of the village belles, ya had to go to church. At least for a little while!

I was settin' over in a dark corner with the rest of the young blades, and as the music was about to start and Miss Effie had struck a chord on the organ, Ole Spendthrift and Mrs. Spendthrift made their entrance and set down in their favorite pew about halfway down the aisle from the front to the back.

After the usual amount of singin' and prayin' the preacher got up, and before he read from the Holy Word, he had a very stern statement to make about the horrible experience that the young ladies and Miss Effie had been subjected to by the uncontrollable brutes in Drippin' Springs Canyon. He elaborated in very sanctified tones on the ill state of affairs in a community when any decent member of society would keep wild cattle that were a threat to the life and limb of the young people who so much wished to enjoy the wonders of the great outdoors where they could enjoy God's handiwork.

Ole Spendthrift set there and turned pink. I was settin' to his back a good way, but I could see red run around the top of that white collar.

No sooner than the preacher said "Amen" than half the mothers of the town made to Ole Spendthrift's pew and went to givin' him large pieces of their minds about the danger that he was heapin' onto their children. You could sure see him flinch, his voice got low and scrapy, he brought out a spotless handkerchief and dabbed the sweat from his brow as he tried to give them ever' assurance that these cows would be gotten out of Drippin' Springs Canyon. Up until now, he claimed that he didn't realize that they had actually been a threat to the social activities of the community . . . but ever'body knew that wasn't the truth.

As I started out at the church door with my gal, he called my name in a very dignified voice, and I stopped and waited for him to walk back to where we were standin'. In the most apologetic tone of voice he asked me could I come by the bank in the morning. Well, for once my bankin' business was in pretty good shape, so I told him I'd be by when I came to town.

I tied my horse in the side street the next morning. As I came around the corner of the bank, Ole Spendthrift was lookin' out of the winder watchin' for me. He motioned for me to come in. We set down at his desk; he had one of those nice, big armchairs pulled up in the right

place for me. He started out with some very light conversation about my cow business and my horses and things
that I knew he wasn't interested in, and directly he came
to the point.

He said, "Ben, what would you pay me for those cows
in Drippin' Springs Canyon, range delivery?"

I set and looked at him a few minutes and said,
"Nothin'!"

This was a rare occasion for me. I had money in the
bank to run me through the winter, my grass leases were
paid, I had plenty of good horses, and lots of feed laid
in—it was rather unusual for me to be in this good a
financial condition. And I'as talkin' to a banker that had
some of his business in worse shape than mine, namely,
them wild cows in Drippin' Springs Canyon. Most all the
workin' cowboys in the community had steady jobs or
steady wives (when cowboys marry these young things
they promise them that they will "quit doin'" lots of
things—bronc horses and bad cattle are generally the first
two) or some other legitimate excuse for not botherin'
with that bunch of ole wild cows. So I wasn't afraid of
this deal gettin' away from me, and I thought I'd just
make it as hard on Ole Spendthrift as I could, which was
the way he usually did it to me.

He said, "Now, Ben, you know those cows are worth
$50 a head and there's about twenty head of 'em and half
of 'em have calves big enough to wean, and I know that
you've got the time to catch these cattle and get 'em out
of that pasture and I want it done to get Miss Effie and
the preacher and the rest of the womenfolk in the community, includin' my own wife, off of my back, so I'll ask

you again what would you give for my cows, range delivery?"

I told him that I hadn't planned on spendin' the winter fightin' a bunch of damned ole wild cows and if he
would agree to give me a lease on the pasture, until April
1, I would agree to give him a note for the cows at a
price, but that I wasn't takin' money out of the bank to
spend for cows, range delivery, in the wintertime.

He knew this all made good sense and I could see that
a lot of the starch was gone out of his conversation. He
had his mouth puckered up like a sheep that had just eat
a bitter acorn and he'as scratchin' his jaw, tryin to figger
out how to protec' his interest.

He finally broke the silence by askin' what that figure
per head would be. I got off the subject by askin' him
about the colts on three ole wild mares that was in the
pasture. He said that he didn't know how the mares come
to have colts, that to his certain knowledge there hadn't
been a stud in that pasture in several years (what he
didn't know was that to my certain knowledge I had
turned a stud in the pasture the year before and left him
long enough to be sure the mares were bred . . . figurin'
on buyin' the colts at the right time, and this was it), and
that he didn't think the colts was worth much money; if I
wanted to try to catch 'em he'd sell 'em to me in the deal.
And he came back to askin' me how much per head I'd
give for the cows.

I finally straightened up in the chair, stiffened my
neck, and cleared my voice and sounded just as hard as
anybody's banker when I said, "I'll give $25 a head for
the cows and $10 a head for the calves and colts and any

other cattle that's in the pasture." (He didn't know it, but there was two or three yearlings left in there from last year's calf crop.)

He choked and swallered and scraped his feet on the marble floor, run his hands through what hair he had left and tried to moisten his lips, and in a whipped kind of voice said, "I won't take it."

I smiled and got up and said, "I'm sure glad of that. Good-bye."

He raised up and said, "Don't you 'good-bye' me. Set down in that chair while I make out the note. At least I'll make a little interest out of the deal."

I loafed up and down the street a few minutes and walked in the country café where the usual gathering of cowboys, ole cowmen, and ranchers and the workin' people of the town were gathered for coffee. The grapevine had worked pretty fast. Because I didn't have my Coke half drank when an old-time rancher cleared his voice behind me and said, "Ben, I hear you bought the Drippin' Springs Canyon cattle, range delivery." Some of 'em swallered their hot coffee, others spewed it out, but they all turned and looked at me and you could tell what they'as all thinkin': *How damn crazy can you get?*

People don't understand about cowboys. In the fall when the shippin's all over and before the winter work starts, when young cowboys come to town they go to the pool hall. The middle-aged cowboys take it a little less strenuous and sit down and play dominoes. The sure 'nuff ole-timers that took the range away from the wilds and built the fences and established the ranch headquarters and built the schools and communities, they set mostly in silence and do the listenin' and the thinkin' that's carried on at coffeetime.

The young cowboys whistled and laughed and asked how many horses I'd cripple and who did I think would have little 'nuff sense to ride in that canyon to gather wild cattle besides me. The middle-aged kind of domino-playin' cowboys . . . one of them spoke up and said, "Did you pay cash or did you give a note for 'em?" I told 'em I give a note for 'em. Ever'body laughed again and said anybody that didn't have no more sense than to give a note for range-delivery cattle could pay for all the drinks.

After a few minutes of silence, ole man Alph said, "Ben, ya got any plans about how you gonna trap them cows?"

I'd been a-studyin' about it, and I told him that when we got all these loose-tongued, twentieth-century mani-cured cowboys out of the gatherin', I'd take it up with the old heads. It was five or six of these ole-timers and they all kinda laughed and nodded their heads at me like they was kinda for me. The gal came around and warmed up the coffee a time or two, and the gatherin' finally broke up in one's and two's, and left me settin' there with the mornin' tab. This didn't shock me none. I paid off and went on back to my horse and rode off toward Drippin' Springs Canyon.

Before hard winter set in I made a few wild runs at these ole cows, caught six head by ropin' 'em, then I'd get 'em wrapped around a tree so they couldn't fight my horse, go home and bring a lead steer in and yoke 'em to this lead steer with a big, soft rope and drive 'em one at a time to my home ranch, which was about ten miles. It was a full day's work to catch one cow, get her out of the canyon and to my ranch. This kind of cow-gatherin' was hard on horses and riggin'. Each time I caught a cow I was in for a day's fight.

One pretty Sunday afternoon I propositioned the high-school-size cowboys to help me, with the intention of cuttin' the calves away from the cows and runnin' 'em down the middle of the canyon and out the gate. There was fifteen of these aspirin' young Saturday-night cowboys and we managed to get seven calves and the three colts off of the ole mares out of the pasture and to my home ranch the same day.

That left me fourteen cows and two yearlings in the pasture, and I didn't bother them any for the rest of the winter. There was lotsa grass in the canyon and I didn't especially need that bunch of ole fightin' cows at my ranch to feed through the winter.

I heard a lot of smart talk around the fire all that winter about my cow trade. This wasn't a new experience to me, which never did bring me to tears nor cause me to worry about that note that wasn't due till the first of April. The last of the February grass was green enough and it looked like we were gonna have a good spring, and I knew I'd better catch those ole cows before they got on the mend.

Ole Man Alph had a pasture that joined the canyon pasture on the back side high up on the prairie. I went to him and asked him if I could cut a gate where his fence line cornered with the canyon pasture, which was way out on the bald prairie. I told him that I wanted to build about two good corrals just inside his pasture. We were

settin' on the south side of the drugstore enjoyin' the
afternoon winter sunshine and no one else was listenin' to
our conversation. He said, "Ben, I'll do better'n that.
I've needed some workin' pens in the back side of that
pasture a long time, just about where you're talkin' about,
and I'll build 'em and have 'em ready for your use in
about two weeks."

The ole man was bein' so good about it all that I
nearly choked down. I told him that I'd come over and
help with diggin' the postholes and puttin' up the fence.
He told me that I needn't worry about that, that he had
plenty of hands that was about through with their winter
feedin' and that he'd see that the matter was tended to.

I was in the canyon in a few days and rode up on top
of the ridge and sure enough the corrals were nearly finished and the gates were already cut in the pasture fence.

I had a pen full of young bulls at my ranch that I had
fed all winter and had 'em in good shape to turn out in the
spring when my cows began to calve. These young bulls
had begin to fight and walk the fence and bawl. I took
four young bulls out in the road and grazed them and
drove them very slowly, went around the edge of town
with them, and over to Ole Man Alph's pasture. I got 'em
in the pens just at dark. They were a little jaded and
laid down and spent the night without any commotion.

Next morning Alph loaned me a wagon and team and
some barrels to haul water and feed and let one of his
hands go help me. We spent most of the morning haulin'
alfalfa hay and fresh windmill water and gettin' these
bulls comfortable in one pen for several days' stay. I
wired these new gates shut and tied extra poles across 'em

to be sure that these young bulls couldn't git out, and then I opened the adjoining pen that led out into the Drippin' Springs pasture. I threw two or three bales of alfalfa hay into that pen, too.

Well, like I said, the grass was gettin' green, the bulls had begin to fight, and the cows had begin to bawl, and I was countin' on that bunch of young bulls romancin' them ole cows out of that canyon into that pen.

'Bout the second day after this long drive these bulls had been on, they began to fight and bawl and paw the ground and pitch that alfalfa hay around on their horns.

The first of these ole wild cows came up out of the rim of the canyon and grazed around on the rim of the canyon and mooed a few times and these bulls romanced 'em into comin' up to the corral where they smelled that alfalfa hay.

I was sittin' way back around on the rim of the canyon to the south side where the wind was against me and the cows couldn't hear nor smell me or my horse. There were five cows in sight; in about an hour's time they worked their way into the corral. They would smell through the fence and rub noses with the bulls between bites of that alfalfa hay. I rode my horse in a slow walk around the rim of the canyon until I got even with the gate. Then I broke him into a dead run, swung the gate closed on five head of wild cows!

Late that afternoon I rode into town and went to Alph's house and told him what I had done. He said, "I'll have the boys bring some gentle cattle to the corrals in the morning and we'll drive those wild cows with 'em to my ranch headquarters, where we can keep 'em until you catch the rest of 'em, and that way you and bulls can open the trap gate again."

In less than a week I had trapped all these cows and Alph had 'em all in the corral at his ranch. We'd kinda kept this business a secret between us.

On Saturday mornin' he and I met at the coffee ground, and he informed all the natives that the wild cows were no longer in Drippin' Springs pasture, but there was two fat yearlings left in the pasture and all the would-be cowboys in the community were invited to be out after dinner that day to help catch and butcher these two yearlings so that on Sunday we could have a big barbecue and reopen Drippin' Springs Canyon for the summer social activities.

This all worked out just like he and I had planned, and the whole community turned out on a beautiful spring Sunday afternoon for a big barbecue. The ladies brought bread and potato salad 'n' stuff, and Ole Spendthrift made a big crock of lemonade with about a small sackful of lemons, but he stirred it and served it and that brought the acid content up to where it was enjoyed by all. And Miss Effie broke over far enough to invite me to the spring recital.

Miss Effie, no doubt about it, exerted a bad influence on the community . . . Just, for instance, there were more people at that barbecue that were paying more attention to the way they held their little finger than to the meat they were sticking the fork in. I was afraid she was about to start "culturizing" cowboys so I rolled the barbecue over to one side of my mouth and said, "Shore I'll come . . . what you goin' to serve?"

INCIDENTS OF
TOWN COWBOYIN'

THE MACHINE AGE HAS REACHED A high state of development and the Atomic Age was mentioned for a few years and now this era of human

existence is referred to as the Space Age. In view of the changes in transportation methods brought on by these various developments and by paved streets and fine residential districts, one-way traffic and all the other unnatural means of movement other than walking, cattle are no longer driven in herds through cities or even through small-size towns because of traffic problems. With the almost deathlike danger of running horses on pavement, and most all cattle, horses and other kinds of livestock being transported to the railroads, central markets, between ranches, feed lots, and other locations by trucks, it seems fitting that some historical record should be made concerning the incidents both humorous and dangerous that occurred during the period when cattle were driven by cowboys horseback through towns and cities of any and all sizes. The real reason that this phase of cowboyin' was necessary was because shipping stock pens at railroad points were built close to the town depot, which by necessity or custom was usually near the business district. The more that business districts developed and the more that the residential part of town grew, the worse located the old original shipping stock pens were insofar as getting cattle from the country through town to the stockyards, and the harder it was, when the cattle were shipped in by rail, to drive them from the stock pens through town out to the country.

FAT CATTLE
AND THE MORNING PAPER

One summer morning early, Roy Young, who was foreman of the Lanius Ranch south of Weatherford, and his cowboys had turned out some good fat Hereford two-year-olds that had been fattened in the feed lot at the ranch. They, of course, were frisky and full of steam and Roy started them to town as early as a rider could distinguish the form of a cow brute, hopin' to take advantage of the coolness of the early morning hours.

There were four carloads of these cattle, which would be in rough figures about a hundred and twenty head. Roy had made the trip to town without too much trouble.

In handling fat young cattle, a rider has to ride point, which means in front of the cattle, and hold them back to keep them from traveling too fast. Then two riders ride wing behind the point and on each side of the herd. Usually there are two more riders bringing up the end of the herd and taking time apart riding back point of the herd when it's necessary to move up to keep cattle from turning down crossroads, lanes, and so forth.

All cowboys and ranchers movin' cattle were glad to get extra help to meet the herd at the edge of town to help them through town to the stock pens at the railroad tracks. For a good many of my growin'-up years, I met several herds of cattle a week during shippin' time the days and nights that I happened to be in town. Of course, we cowboys learned and dreaded concrete sidewalks, clotheslines, bicycles, open doors to storm houses and cellars, unprotected water hydrants stickin' up in the yard, and one hundred and one other things too numerous to mention, such as tricycles, little red wagons, squealin' kids, high-tone screamin' old women and damned old grouchy men that lived along the streets where it was necessary to move herds of cattle back and forth to the railroad.

That day me and some more boys met Roy's cattle about early mid-morning at the south edge of town and eased up South Main Street, which at that time was wide and unpaved. When we came to Weatherford College, we turned the cattle east a block and then north onto the street that would run into the railroad tracks close to the stock pens.

Nothing eventful happened until we were over on this street and hardly a mile from the stock pens. Then old Judge Irving, who was settin' on the porch readin' the morning paper, saw the cattle comin' up the street. For fear that there might be a cow track put on his lawn, he walked up to the edge of the porch and shook that morning newspaper unfurled and hollered "Houey" a couple of times.

Roy turned in his saddle and saw the stampede started and he knew that the run was on and that we would have cattle scattered for the rest of the day. But before he left Judge Irving's, he rode over in the yard horseback, jerked the paper out of Judge Irving's hand, folded it and handed it back to him and said, "Judge, these cattle don't want to read the damn paper, they want to go to the stock pens, so take it in the house with you and stay there."

HEIFERS YEARNIN' FOR HIGHER LEARNIN'

One morning we had turned out three hundred and twenty long yearling Angus heifers and started out of town with them to what was known as the Black Ranch. We were about even with the college campus in that narrow street and were ready to turn and get onto South

Main Street, which was much wider and easier to work up and down the side of a herd of cattle to keep them out of the yards and from goin' down cross streets.

As we swung the leaders on the point and were about halfway around the corner with the herd, some college girls came runnin' out of the dormitory squealin' and hollerin' and takin' on about the cattle and they sounded like a cross between a glee club and a pep rally. All this sudden commotion and high female voices had a nerve-rackin' effect on this bunch of black heifers that had been shipped four or five days and were thirsty, hungry, and nervous and unused to such commotion, and so the stampede was on. I'm sure the college girls thought it was most colorful.

It looked like a big bunch of these big black heifers were about to 'tend class when I cut them off and only two topped the college steps and started through the hall. I jerked my feet out of the stirrups and sat keep in my saddle, in case ole Beauty might fall on that slick oiled floor, and went through the college hallway.

There was a one-armed, narrow-eyed preacher that was a teacher in the college and he had some other things about him that was empty besides that sleeve on his shirt. As me and Beauty made the intersection of the two hallways and turned this heifer toward an open door on the other end of the hallway, this preacher waved that empty sleeve at me and screamed in a high, sanctimonious tone of voice that I didn't have to ride that horse in there. I hollered back at him as we went back into the sunlight that the reason I did it was that I was afraid that the heifer might get in the wrong class.

CLOTHESLINES,
COWBOYS,AND PETTICOATS

One morning Jack Hart, who was a good cowman and village banker and had a feed lot two or three miles north of town, turned out a bunch of steers at the stock pens to go to the feed lot. There were several good cowhands helpin' on this quick, short drive and the north side of Weatherford wasn't as hard to get through with a herd as the south side was. However, this bunch of big steers decided to make a pretty wild run.

They weren't gettin' away. We were managin' to hold 'em up the road we wanted them on, but ever'body was jumpin' sidewalks and curbs—which was dangerous horseback and runnin' through yards—and one cowboy made a wild dash around through the back yard. He dodged a loaded clothesline almost, but his horse had broke into and begun to buck because, when he raised his head up comin' out from under the clothesline, he had fitted himself with a beautiful lacy, frilled petticoat right around his neck, and I guess this old pony didn't like petticoats. He bucked into that herd of steers and we had the damnest runaway that a bunch of cowboys ever had.

This cowboy was sorta known as a ladies' man, and after he had shed his petticoat and we had got the herd sort of herded back together about even with the oil mill, Jack rode by him and said, "I never thought that you would get trapped by an *empty* petticoat."

COTTON HEAD IN THE SANDBOX

We were movin' three hundred head of big steers through Denton one time and I was ridin' point. These cattle were travelin' in kind of a long, sweepin' trot. They weren't exactly wild, but they were a little excited and travelin' pretty fast and I saw that they were goin' to turn on a side street where we didn't want them to go. It was on a corner and I took a short cut around through the back yard of a home to head them off.

This back yard had a big rosebush hedge around it about four feet tall. I was ridin' a good fast horse and he came to that hedge and rose and jumped it and then I saw that near where we were landin' on the other side there was a cute little bitty cotton-headed kid playin' in a sandbox.

The sandbox was built up a foot or so and made it easy for me to bend down and take a hold of him. I knew some cattle or more cowboys might have to come that way, and just as my horse's forefeet hit the ground real close to this little fellow, I reached down and picked him up by one arm. A young woman screamed and came runnin' out the back door.

I don't know how old this kid was, but he wasn't much heavier than a feed of oats. I'd be no judge of young stock and I don't know whether he was weaned or still a-suckin', but, anyway, I just picked him up by one arm, and as I rode by and handed him to his mother he was likin' the ride through the air and gave me a big smile.

I said, "Mama, grow him up some more and I'll take him with me next time." I never knew whether she fainted or got in the house with him.

During the worst days of the now historical depression, I bought one hundred and twenty-seven cows. These were good-quality cattle and they had about sixty-two calves on 'em. They were a little old, they had some horns and wrinkles on their horns, but they weren't bad cattle at all, and I gave $12.50 a head for them and the calves throwed in for nothin'. I kept this herd of cattle way late in the fall and finally sold them without makin' much money, but that's not the story. We were drivin' this herd of cows through Mineral Wells on horseback down one of the main residential streets started south toward the Brazos River.

There was kind of a snobbish fellow that had a real nice home with a big lawn and rosebushes; it was a well-kept place. Cowboys didn't have a whole lot of use for him. He was sort of a small loanshark, and as far as we were concerned he wasn't one of God's most noble children; but, nevertheless, we were tryin' to get the cattle through town with the least possible trouble. I was ridin' point and wing on the side by his house, and I was doin' my best to keep the cattle out of his yard.

We had nearly passed his yard when he came from around the corner of the house with a big, bold, fuzzy black dog followin'; he got right up close and, with a big grin on his face, said in a loud tone of voice, "Sic 'em!"

Well, these old cattle didn't sic 'em too good. They weren't wild. They were a gentle kind of cattle, but this dog nipped the heels of a calf that let out a little hurt kind of bawl, and the old cow turned around and, with that duly amount of horn she had grown in her lifetime, she hooked and knocked a chunk of black hair off the dog. With him out of the way, she took after this old man, and the calf was runnin' after them too. They ran round the house.

The man had a little outbuilding with his yard tools and stuff in it and the door was open, and that old cow was crowdin' him so fast that he just kinda climbed up that door and got on top of the little building. It was about six-by-six and maybe six or seven feet tall, and there he was on top of it and this old cow was a-runnin' around it by the time I got back there.

Well, the little calf was bewildered and dived into that opened door and was standin' in there in the dark a-bawlin'; the old cow could hear it bawl but she didn't know what happened to it, so she was just goin' round and round that little shed shakin' her horns and pawin' dirt and throwin' it over her back. I knew that when the calf turned around and saw daylight and listened to that old cow a minute she would come back out.

So I was just a-sittin' there on my horse a-watchin' the show. Mr. Loanshark was on top of his little building and turned white as a sheet and he finally realized I was sittin' out there on my horse and he asked, "What are you goin' to do to get this cow away from here?"

I was really waitin' for the little calf to make up his mind to come out of the shed, but I just said to the cow, "Sic 'em!"

WHEN BIG STEERS
CLEARED THE WAY

The Fort Worth Stock Packers were out of beef in the winter of 1929 and 1930 because of the extreme cold weather, and cattle feeders weren't shipping anything to Forth Worth. Swift and Company, buyer for big steers, called Fred Smith long-distance in Weatherford and offered him a two-cents-a-pound premium if he could send them some heavy finished beef.

Fred came down to the wagonyard to the old camp house. All wagonyards in those days had a good, tight camp house, generally with two rooms in it and a fireplace in each room for people who were travelin' in wagons to camp in during bad weather. On bad days the cowboys, traders, and loafers would gather in the camp house and keep up a big fire and a lot of big conversation and maybe play some dominoes, so Fred knew where to find the cowboys at that time of day in that kind of weather.

He told us his troubles and he thought he could get seventy-two cattle cut out, which would be three carloads of twenty-four to the car, if we thought we could get them to town. Fred had one man at the feed lot and there were four of us there that thought we could go, so we told him we didn't know whether we could get to town with them or not because the streets were solid ice. Anywhere a horse had to travel, you were subject to slip and fall. There was some fine sleet in the air while we were talking.

We put on all the clothes we had and heavy chaps and big leather coats. Most of us had a horse or two in the wagonyard, so we saddled our favorite horses and went out to the feed lot, which was about three miles from the stock pens in town. These cattle were all fat, so Fred just opened the gate and counted out seventy-two head that he hoped we could drive to town.

As he turned them out of the small feed lot that these cattle had been kept in, he turned them into a little trap pasture. Cattle as fat as that can get out on hard ground and fresh air and feel good, so these cattle romped and bucked and played and we didn't try to hold them up. We thought we would kinda let them get their play out because they weren't scared. They were just doin' it for fun and they would quit in a few minutes without hurtin' anything. When they began to blow a lot of steam out and slow up a little bit, we opened the gate out onto the road. A couple of boys went out to ride point and hold them down the best they could goin' up the lane, and me and another cowboy brought up the herd. Nearly all the streets were solid ice and there was no traffic. Nobody was in the way but it was an awful hard way to try to move cattle, especially fat cattle that were rollicky and feelin' good.

All of us either stood in our stirrups or rode with our feet out of the stirrups for fear our horse would fall with us. When you are ridin' standin' in your stirrups and you have one hand on your reins and another on your saddle horn, if a horse starts to fallin' you can kinda stiff-arm yourself out of the saddle with one hand, and if you are ridin' with that hand on the saddle you are ready all the time. The other way, ridin' settin' down in your saddle with both feet out of the stirrups, you are countin' on goin' down with the horse. By having your feet loose, you won't get caught with a leg under your horse and you will be free to roll on the ground away from him to safety. When I rode on ice and slick pavement, this was the way that I did it, and in spite of my many injuries, I have never had my foot caught in the stirrup under a horse.

We came down Elm Street headed north to the stock yards. Fort Worth Street ran east and west and the Weatherford Post Office was on the corner where Fort Worth Street took a sudden drop at the point we were crossin' these cattle. This herd of big cattle began to slip and slide and fall. The seventy-two head had piled up in the middle of Fort Worth Street, not tryin' to get away but because they just couldn't stand up.

We cowboys didn't dare try to hurry our horses as they were scotchin' to try to keep from fallin'. We stood there all around these cattle a-cussin', cryin', and hollerin' and wavin' our hands at them but wonderin' how we were even goin' to get them up on their feet.

These big stout cattle would scuffle and struggle and then give up because they couldn't get a footing to stand up. We managed to ride closer to them and holler louder at 'em. The fine sleet in the air was freezin' on our clothes and freezin' on the manes and tails of our horses, but these big steers were so hot and full of rich feed that the sleet would melt as it would hit them.

Now here is the historical part of the story, something that I never saw happen before in my lifetime and I doubt seriously if it will ever happen again, at least in Texas, because we never drive cattle this way any more: the body heat of those seventy-two steers piled up on that solid frozen pavement began to soften the surface of the ice enough that, when they began to try to get up again, their feet held in the soft ice. They melted the ice with their own bodies enough to be able to get back up on their feet, and we rode our horses across a sort of a mush that was a lot better than being on solid ice.

It was about three fourths of a mile on down to the stock pens and these cattle then were so scared of their footing that none of them ever tried to run or get away, and we drove them down to the stock pens without any more trouble. The railroad spotted the cars and we loaded the cattle just at dark and sealed the car doors and went to town.

We went into the Texas Café and back to the stove in the back side of the dining part. We pulled off our horse-hide coats and our chaps and there was so much ice on them that they stood up on the floor after we were out of 'em. It made a loblolly, but Florent Patrick and Little Pat and all was glad to see us get warm and glad to know that we got the steers shipped and nobody got any chousin' about gettin' water on the floor from thawin' out the clothes. Somebody just got a mop and cleaned it up and was glad that we were back in town and nobody hurt.

STEERS THAT
STOOD WATCH

IN THE SPRING OF 1937 THE CATTLE business had showed considerable recovery from the days of the depression. However, cattle prices still weren't very high, but there was a marginal difference in the price of feeder and stocker cattle and fat cattle. Steermen that hadn't found any cure for it were goin' back into big steers and it was time to ship big steers from South Texas to the Osage grass country of northern Oklahoma and the Flint Hills of Kansas. The economic recovery and the American taste for beef had changed the demand some for big, heavy grass-fed cattle, but "steermen" were an old and diehard part of the cowboy game and were trying to hang on to the only way that some of them knew to handle cattle. I was a young man but had the same feeling about the steer business that many of the old-timers did. It was still the easiest and most enjoyable way to handle and sell finished cattle.

The last week in April I shipped two hundred and seventy-eight head of three- and four-year-old steers and unloaded them at Pawhuska, Oklahoma. We drove northeast from Pawhuska to near the headwaters of Bird Creek and Buck Creek, where I had made arrangements to graze these cattle through the summer. Four hundred miles north from South Texas was still a little chilly in late April but there had been plenty of real good rain and bluestem sage grass had begun to put out for spring.

My stompin' ground to loaf and buy chuck supply for my camp was the little town of Foraker. I had a good camp under a big old shed that was once built to store hay in and was boxed in on the north and open on three sides. This was one of the best summers that I ever spent out in a camp summerin' a bunch of steers. It rained every time it should to make the grass grow, the sun came out right behind the rains, and we didn't have any weather that would have been termed "bad" all through the summer.

Big steers will get fat on bluestem or other good grazin' in the summertime because they have enough growth that their frame is mature and what they graze will turn into good, firm beef. The market was steady and even went up a little and I began to ship these cattle and I would cut out three or four carloads of the fattest ones. We shipped cattle every week in September and had about finished when we had a hard killin' frost in October. Cattle will not put on any more flesh after frost and the grass dries up and loses a lot of its food value.

I had a remnant of twenty-one steers not fattened as good as the rest of the herd. There were a few big fat steers in the bunch that every time we rounded up and cut some to ship, these few big cattle had managed to get away. There were two big yellow steers with a little brindle along their sides that had been hard to hold in the roundup when I had shipped out of South Texas, and these two were still the ringleaders of the ones that had been gettin' away. The pasture was mostly open in high rollin' hills and valleys. However, there was a considerable amount of brush along the headwaters of Bird Creek and these cattle had begun to hide out over there on water and in that thicket. I had a good Okie farm boy that was makin' a cowhand helpin' me, and after we had shipped the last several cars of steers, we started out in dead earnest to get this remnant, which would be about a carload.

The first morning we saw a big yellow steer high on the ridge, and I said to Okie, "The rest of them will be just over that ridge grazin' on the slope."

We dropped down below them, which would be

south, and we intended to drive them north to the corral of this pasture. We were half a mile from that big yellow steer, and he was lookin' west and we were ridin' south and acted like we didn't see him, but that didn't fool him none. He bawled real loud, shook his head, and wrung his tail and ran down the slope to signal, and the whole herd dived in the brush just about the time we got in sight of them.

We worked and hollered and rode through the brush across the creek and back and forth, and it was just rough enough for us and our horses that cattle could turn back and get by us. We made about three hard drives at them with no luck. I hollered at Okie to meet me at the head of the draw and we worked our way out of the brush. By this time the morning was gone, so we went back to camp to fix a batch of grub for dinner. It was not hot weather and it didn't hurt to try to work these cattle anytime during the day. However, they were fat and I wanted to get them to the stock pens fat and I wasn't interested in makin' a week's or ten days' long, hard chousin' cow-workin' on this last carload of steers.

That afternoon we found these cattle way over on the east fence line in the open and we were ridin' up behind them from the valley through the slope when that other big yellow steer came out of the creek bottom from behind the water and in front of us, runnin' at top tilt and ran into the herd that was grazin', and the race was on. Of course, they got back in the thicket on us and we were no better off than before we had started early that morning.

Big, grass-fed, fat, crossbred, motley-faced brindle

steers are wise and fresh and discourage a cowboy from droppin' a loose rope around everything he sees movin'. I sure didn't feel like it would be smart to rope these steers one at a time and jerk and pull my horses the way they would have to to handle them, and worse than that it would cause lots of shrink and loss of weight on these cattle; but these big aged steers had learned to like that blue grass and didn't intend to give up easy. I realize now that during the other times that we rounded up this pasture and shipped fat steers that these two yellow steers and that little herd they were with had worked themselves out a signal system, and they stood watch either from front or back or from side to side of the rest of the herd against the chance of any cowboys sneakin' up on them. Before we went to sleep I rustled through my personal belongin's and found a big, half-circle horse doctor's needle that I usually carried to sew up a cut horse with. You might not need it but once a year, and you hoped that you never would when you were camped out workin' stock.

Next morning early we could see high on the ridge one of these big yellow steers standing watch, and I said to Okie, "let's catch him before he gets to the herd."

When we really took after this old steer it sort of surprised him. I guess he was used to cowboys tryin' to head him and he didn't think about one followin' and ropin' him. I was ridin' a good fast grey horse that could sure put me up for a loop at this big set of horns. I pitched a big blocker loop on him and caught him around the head and over one horn, and the rope took up right over his windpipe. The best way in the world to catch a sure-enough fat steer is to rope and choke him at the windpipe right at the point of the throat and put the rope between the horns so it won't slip down his neck to where there is a lot of hide and flesh wadded up between his windpipe and your rope. This big stout grey horse couldn't throw the steer, but he was doin' a good job of shuttin' off his wind.

I had put Okie on a horse called Charlie and he was workin' fast, doing his best to pick up this old steer's hind feet with a rope, and I drug this big steer around and got him choked and as he moved his back legs, sure enough, Okie finally got his rope high up about even with his hocks and we pulled him down on the ground. Both these horses had experience in headin' and heelin' big steers.

I rubbed old Charlie on the hip and talked to him and pulled a hair out of his tail about eighteen inches long. I had stuck my crooked needle in the flap of my shirt pocket. I threaded this needle with that stout black horsehair and Okie got a death grip on this old steer's horns and turned his nose up like a cowboy bulldoggin' a steer. I proceeded to sew his eyelids together with the horsehair. Of course, he offered a more than reasonable amount of objection, but I had a horse holdin' on each end of him and a stout farmboy that was fast becomin' a cowboy holdin' his head. It took about thirty minutes to shut out the daylight to where his watch duty was gonna be about over. We took our rope off and let him up and he stood there, wrung his tail, shook his head, and bawled. There was hardly any blood made by this needle and he had no reason to complain on the grounds of pain, but it was the fact that he couldn't *see all* and *know all* that was makin' him mad. He very cautiously eased off down the draw, smellin' and bawlin' and hopin' to find the rest of the herd, but he didn't run into them and scatter them. As we rode closer, that other big yellow steer came from across the creek on the other slope and ran into the middle and, by himself, led them into the thicket. We just rode back to camp and rested until after dinner and waited for them to come out.

We had ridden to the other low side of the creek where it ran under the fence and worked our way around until we could see the color of cattle in the thicket. We stayed there a long time and talked and visited in a low tone of voice and drew pictures of various kinds of brands in the dirt with the end of a broomweed and passed the time like cowboys generally do when waitin' out stock.

It was late afternoon when this other big yellow steer eased out ahead of the herd to take watch on the ridge and he was surprised when we cut him off from the herd and ran him uphill and paid no attention to the rest of the herd. He was a little faster—maybe I was a little slower— and we ran him a little farther, but this time Okie got a throw at his head and I got his hind feet and we stretched him out quick. I pulled another horsehair and threaded my needle and made a nice little hemstitchin' job on both of his eyelids. We took the rope off and rode away and left him here. It was almost dusk.

Next morning after good sunup we managed to get in behind this bunch of cattle and cut them off from the brush. This pair of big yellow steers were by far the biggest and walkin' the nicest behind the herd, which was the only way they had figured they could drift. They could smell and hear the cattle in front of them. The rest of these cattle really weren't very wild. These old big steers had been leadin' them astray.

When we got them in the stock pens, which were big and high and stout, with the shipping gates fastened, I put these two big steers in a branding chute, put a rope on their horns, and pulled their heads up tight to a post. With a small pocketknife I cut the horsehair and let their eyes loose and knew that they were glad to see daylight, but I am sure they didn't exactly appreciate their surroundings.

A NOTE
ABOUT THE AUTHOR

Ben K. Green, whose *Horse Tradin'* is already a minor classic at the very least in a rich assemblage of Western Americana, is the kind of a Westerner who almost crawled out of the cradle and into a saddle, spending his childhood, adolescence, and young manhood horseback. He studied veterinary medicine in the United States and abroad and practiced in the Far Southwest in one of the last big horse counties in North America. When he eventually gave up his practice and research, he returned to Cumby, Texas, where he now lives, raising good horses and cattle.

A NOTE
ON THE TYPE

The text of this book was set on the Linotype in a new face called Primer, designed by Rudolph Ruzicka, earlier responsible for the design of Fairfield and Fairfield Medium, Linotype faces whose virtues have for some time now been accorded wide recognition.

The complete range of sizes of Primer was first made available in 1954, although the pilot size of 12 point was ready as early as 1951. The design of the face makes general reference to Linotype Century (long a serviceable type, totally lacking in manner or frills of any kind) but brilliantly corrects the characterless quality of that face.

This book was composed, printed, and bound by The Haddon Craftsmen, Inc., Scranton, Pa. Typography and binding design by Bonnie Spiegel.